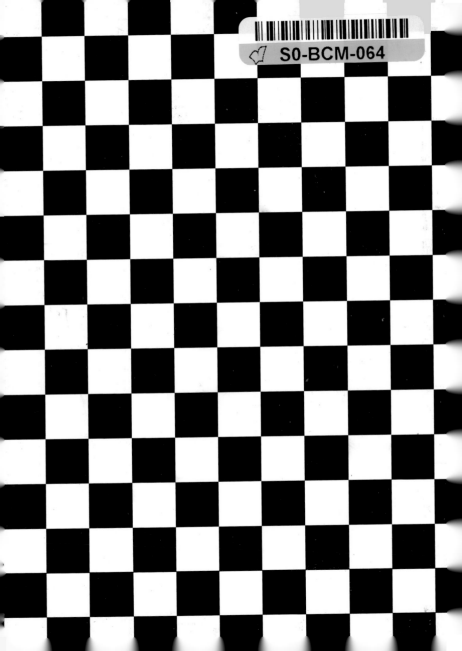

S0-BCM-064

"There are only two ways to live your life.
One is as though nothing is a miracle.
The other is as though everything is a miracle."

- Albert Einstein -

The Jetstream of Success

Julian Pencilliah

Contents

INTELLECTUAL MAVERICK

I was fortunate enough to realise that life requires more than a whisper of wisdom. It seems as though it unfolds like a tapestry of magic that orchestrates its opulent wonder. People have always been my source of inspiration, which has allowed me to discover a world within myself, and beyond my world. I've been privileged to have incredible adventures across the world, all of which have truly opened my eyes to a wealth of knowledge, and broadened my perspective in ways that were both humbling and enlightening.

I've experienced acts of kindness in the most improbable places and circumstances that would have moved even the most jaded of souls. I've witnessed the human spirit's willingness to challenge and rise above the most seemingly impossible odds.

We all journey through life experiencing highs and lows, and at times we may feel as though the cards are stacked against us.

But irrespective of the hand we've been dealt, we should never allow ourselves the luxury of self-defeating mentalities. I've written *The Jetstream of Success* in gratitude to the thousands of people who have inspired me.

The design of the chapters will offer you the insight necessary for you to avoid major setbacks. It will also provide you with the emotional, intellectual and analytical disciplines to frame greater successes.

I live by three simple words: compassion, love and gratitude. We need to act on these three words daily. Doing so will irrevocably change our world.

INTELLECTUAL MAVERICK

The Pinnacle of Success

The Pinnacle of Success
Irrevocably change your world

Imagine a journey
that leaves you awestruck with
a child-like wonder. . . .

INTELLECTUAL
MAVERICK

A journey that causes you to irrevocably change your world. Imagine a journey that ignites the magic of you, leaving you in awe of your sheer magnificence. It is one that can piece together an ever-fuller understanding of yourself, articulating a quest to define and re-define monumental discoveries within your potential, allowing you to become more acutely aware as time passes.

23:53:09¼
TO YOUR PODIUM FINISH

INTELLECTUAL MAVERICK

A journey that will expand your thought into uncharted dimensions; one that will take you to a place where heaven embraces the earth; where your soul touches your humanity.

There are eternal truths that have been apparent from lifetimes before, and will be apparent for lifetimes to come. These truths oscillate as jet streams, pulsating throughout every culture across the world.

I invite you to embark on a journey with me, a journey of self-discovery. This journey will reveal infinite truths through the illusiveness of your psyche; truths that are even unknown to the author and can only be discovered through you from moment to moment.

The text is meant to be an oscillating transparency, revealing you to yourself, and bringing about monumental change while awakening your greatest instinct to progress exponentially through multi-dimensional time frames. It's based on the realisation that the richest awakening of yourself will unveil life's deepest mysteries.

When your back is up against the wall, and your thought is all you've got, that thought becomes your journey and that journey can become the story of your life.

So we begin this unveiling of your destiny with recognition of the legend within you. . . .

Legends create history everyday. The status of being a Legend is reserved for the chosen few who believe they are destined for greatness.

INTELLECTUAL MAVERICK

INTELLECTUAL
MAVERICK

The Jetstream of Success is an accelerated experience of life. It is living on the edge of possibility, living through a pulsation and a passion. It's a place of wonder, in the discovery that truth is infinite. It's being in focused motion and a master of the speed of intention.

Anyone who has reached the pinnacle in their arena of success has slipped into the *Jetstream*, which established their miraculous rate of achievement. Consider the rate of achievement of a person who literally goes from rags to billionaire in a lifetime. And then again, there are those who become self-made billionaires in less than a decade. Whether it's in the arena of sport, entertainment, business or any other success, the constant factor with these super achievers is always the rate of achievement.

When we stand afar and look at these super achievers, we see their efforts, we see their strategies, and we see their talents. However, what we don't see is the relationship that these achievers have with themselves, and that quality is the fabric of this rate of achievement.

The performance of these super achievers is directly relative to their psychology.

INTELLECTUAL MAVERICK

The Jetstream of Success has been designed to navigate you through the dynamics of your performance psychology so that you will engage the legend within you.

INTELLECTUAL MAVERICK

Legends have the capacity to employ their genius and awaken their brilliance. They exhibit a conscious clarity and focus towards the recognition of their intentions and the refinement of their aptitude. Your potential to awaken these qualities is infinite, as is your potential to unveil the experience of your greatest success.

In fact, your legend may be in the vastness of the eternal continuum of the now, but it's also a passage. It's your prime rite of passage; a passage of discovery and achievement. A passage through a sequence of rhythms of life. A passage through choreography of opportunity and a symphony of circumstances that's meant to be orchestrated like magic.

The magic of you is in your capacity to *shape change.*

The magic of you is in your capacity to transcend life's most erratic terrain and to associate with the value of celebration. Imagine for a boundless second, a journey through your celebrations. A stitching of insights into intentions of focus, an unveiling of experience.

To irrevocably change your world is to gain the flexibility to see the moment as it presents itself. It's establishing a position on your awareness. This is achieved by a meditative interpretation of your life, which is a crystallisation of your awareness from the depth of your being.

To awaken this mental faculty, *The Jetstream of Success* will take you into the largeness of opportunity within the dimension of humour. It's within the dimension of humour that the generosity to indulge in the lighter side of life is illuminated.

INTELLECTUAL MAVERICK

UNVEIL YOUR DESTINY

INTELLECTUAL
MAVERICK

So now, let us journey into some of the most compromising analogies, and get a grip on the process of interpretation. Let's take a magic carpet ride to a place within your awareness, where the vastness of the potential within you is realised.

"ANY MAN WHO CAN DRIVE SAFELY WHILE KISSING A PRETTY GIRL IS SIMPLY NOT GIVING THE KISS THE ATTENTION IT DESERVES."

- ALBERT EINSTEIN -

Take the Reins

Take the Reins
Place a rein on your intentions

We all learn our lessons in life. I learned one of my most valuable lessons when I was a teenager, taking my girlfriend horseback riding. I can smile at the humour of it now, but on that particular day, I was left speechless with embarrassment.

I find a hidden treasure of a place to go horseback riding; a nature reserve overlooking the Indian Ocean. As we arrive, our guides welcome us with wide, friendly smiles. They proudly tell us we're about to ride ex-July horses - the Rothmans July was one of the biggest horse racing events in the world.

Announcing himself, one of the stallions snorts as he pounds the ground with his hoof.

"That one's yours," says my guide, grinning and nodding at me.

20:37.22³⁶

TO YOUR PODIUM FINISH

A knot begins to form in my stomach, and my knees buckle a little as I realise what I've gotten myself into.

We are introduced to our horses. My horse's name is Chester; he's white and grey, standing tall with distinct pride. My girlfriend's horse is Blackjack, seemingly the more playful one, neighing and nudging at Chester from time to time. I feel my mouth become strangely dry as I notice Chester glancing at me with a contemptuous pleasure.

Nevertheless, I turn around to my girlfriend and give her a reassuring smile. My smile weakens as I feel the damp heat of the horse's breath on my neck. I swiftly turn around; Chester looks somewhat amused. Reluctantly, I draw a deep breath and mount the horse; my girlfriend observes and follows my lead.

Firmly seated upon Chester, I heave a sigh of relief as we start to trot at a comfortable pace.

INTELLECTUAL MAVERICK

I glance around and begin to appreciate the beauty of my surroundings. The ocean, a cool azure, glistens in the sunlight. The horse's hooves gently splash in the waves as they sink into the golden sand.

EVERYTHING IS PERFECT.

INTELLECTUAL MAVERICK

Then, as we approach a bend, we come in sight of a grassy plain. This psychologically triggers the horses into thinking they are in training. Instantly, both stallions take-off into a full gallop, racing through the field. The guide instinctively goes after my girlfriend's horse and manages to grab hold of the reins, assuming that I, being the confident rider I said I was, would take care of myself.

Despite my efforts, I lose all control of the horse; I'm overwhelmed with fear and couldn't be in a more compromising position.

"Whoa Chester! Take it easy, we're a team, work with me," I plead.

Ignoring me as though he has selective hearing, Chester gallops harder with tremendous speed and power.

My fists tighten as I pull harder on the reins in a desperate attempt to bring him to a halt; my efforts totally in vain.

My mind screams in a manner that could move the foundations of hell. My voice constricts with emotion as it shifts from coaxing to screams of terror. My ego spirals downwards to the very core of the earth.

I ask myself, "What could this horse possibly have against me?"

INTELLECTUAL MAVERICK

Was this karma's way of getting me to pay for the sum of all my sins for a hundred lifetimes? What have I done to offend this horse, or more so, the Gods of crude humour? As Chester races on defiantly, I feel my face turn a deep shade of red. The horse is now running into a valley where I am still in full view of my girlfriend. Eventually, to my relief, he begins to slow down to a controllable pace. It is then that I feel the full impact of my humiliation.

I feel a strained smile creep onto my face as I try to salvage the pieces of my crushed ego. My mind begins racing as to how I can overcome the embarrassment of being caught out. It is then that Chester decides to take one final dig at my pride; he bends over to have a drink of water, and since the human tendency is to lean backwards, which I do. But in doing so, I lose my balance, and grasp onto the horse's rear!

Okay! So I may have exaggerated the story a little for the purpose of making an entertaining read, however, there is a very valuable lesson that comes out of it.

LIFE REQUIRES MORE THAN A WHISPER OF WISDOM.

You see, the mind is not a noun; it is merely a process, a process of trains of thought that direct your life. It is the nature of the mind to experience thought, be it intended or unintended. The problem being that not all thoughts support your efforts to materialise your dreams. WE NEED TO SEE OUR COLLECTIVE MIND AS THE VEHICLE THAT WILL TAKE US TO THE *DESTINY* OF OUR DREAMS.

INTELLECTUAL MAVERICK

Even as I now realise the importance of the technique of manipulating the reins to direct and control a horse, in the same fashion, we need to realise that there is a technique behind harnessing the power of the mind. Just as the horse is kept on a path by the reins, likewise we need to introduce or create reins for the mind. We need to ensure that it is tamed and trained, to never dilute our intentions with thoughts of a weak or destructive nature.

ENGINEER CHANGE

So, if to live successfully just required mind auditing between negative and positive thoughts, then why do we act as though we and our loved ones are going to live forever? Why does most of society get caught up, sometimes for years, in anger, jealousy, sadness and hurt?

Honestly, who has the time for these self-defeating mentalities? To the best of my knowledge, we are only here for one lifetime. Don't eclipse your sun by not understanding the value of time.

The skill of applying intellect to every aspect of your life is a bridge that everyone has to cross, and that bridge is called awareness. Yogis spend a lifetime achieving this elevation of grand awareness, and this is the journey that I am suggesting we take daily.

THERE'S JUST ONE PROBLEM.

Inevitably, you will go through life only to discover that you are your own greatest enemy. The evidence of which can be found in the following:

Clinical Psychology

Clinical psychology suggests that we have no conscious experience of the various mental processes that constitute our day. Our thinking should be a part of a mental process that is more consciously conducive to our intentions. When we experience thoughts that are random or disorderly, then we become severed from the mental processes that are conducive to our intentions. We have to bring an order, structure and dimension into our everyday awareness.

Just do It!
Hell no!

Our actions range between our conscious competence and unconscious incompetence. To live successfully, we should always mitigate our risks comprehensively, and for this reason, evaluating our risks should always be our first priority.

INTELLECTUAL MAVERICK

ENGINEER CHANGE

INTELLECTUAL MAVERICK

We need to evaluate the merits of the risk associated to the action or inaction before seeking any returns. We should never have a confident approach if we are unaware of our level of competence. Most people are unrealistic about their unconscious incompetence and as a result, tend to be bull-headed in their tendency to pursue opportunities that don't make sense from a process and/or execution perspective. We need to become more realistic in the way we define the range between our conscious competence and unconscious incompetence in each situation.

Our capacity
to more fully evaluate
our capability
and
incapability

will reduce our odds of experiencing losses.

Character

Does your intellect employ your character, or does your character employ your intellect? The natural order of your being is: innocence, as it is framed in love, then contribution, compassion and gratitude. The problem being, when we factor ourselves in the outer world, we experience conflicts of psychologies between our intentions, anticipated results, and our expectations of people in the world. Those conflicts of interest will, as a result, quicken our reaction into anger, jealousy, hurt or fear. If your character exhibits these poor qualities then the results you seek will become synchronistic with these qualities. Make every effort to keep at the forefront of your awareness that your character always employs your intellect. Your intellect is only an engine that executes the resonance of your character, so introduce into your life acts and thoughts of love, compassion, gratitude and contribution as daily rituals.

INTELLECTUAL MAVERICK

ENGINEER CHANGE

Engineering Change

INTELLECTUAL MAVERICK

Living is really about engineering change through the exhilaration of possibility. We need to shape our circumstance and influence the outcomes, bringing them into a dynamic coherence, launching these ideas into exponential achievement. However, we all have biases in our mental processes that can distort and tarnish our intentions. Negative biases are generally a result of a limited insight, a weak mental muscle, fear, and any thoughts that prevent us from investigating potential. We need to place our emphasis on defining the result we wish to achieve and its execution.

Value of Life

One of the greatest difficulties that society faces is that we don't know how to place a value on the things that matter most. We are so preoccupied in our daily lives with trivial acquisitions that are normally associated with price tags that we tend not to recognise and value the things that really matter. Typical examples of these are your health, relationships, spiritual development and sophisticated thinking processes. We need to define what matters most.

When you consider your life's path and the decades before you, you will find that life is going to demand a lot of you in terms of your capabilities to move forward incrementally. You will not be allowed the luxury of any self-defeating mentality.

INTELLECTUAL MAVERICK

In fact, on the contrary, you have to be constantly thinking on your feet, and when you do experience a setback, you have to hit the ground running.

You will need to know when to be assertive and wise enough to know when to exercise patience.

You will need to demonstrate the courage to overcome even your most wounding critics.

But most importantly, you will need to take the definitive, intelligent action to create the composition of your life's successes without placing self-inflicted excuses, such as lack of expertise, education or financial backing or any other excuse that stands between you and your successes.

It sounds like a tall order, but you have to be sure to deliver. The question is, do you think that your mind is capable of holding all of this information with the awareness that warrants intelligent action? Legends create history everyday, and the returns they seek are directly relative to the acquired intelligence that underpins their actions. We all start off in life with minds that are quite fragile and weak in mental activity, until we reach that turning point where we become schooled to the predictive intelligence and spontaneous nature of our successes.

This chapter is intended to help you engineer a life of greater progress by raising your awareness to the power of intelligence.

INTELLECTUAL MAVERICK

It seems that in this fast-paced world, our present day intentions lack the shelf life to create future successes, and due to the complex nature of awareness, it's hard to distil and hold the relevancy of our goals. How do we become more wakeful and present to our lives?

The last century has been a culmination of cutting-edge science. Tens of thousands of scientists from Russia, America and India have mobilised in a global effort to rush towards the discovery of an instrument that's meant to serve as a space-time continuum to make us more present in our lives. *The Jetstream* has employed the theories of relativity, astrophysics and quantum mechanics. We beat the scientists out there...we've discovered it...*the diary!* 😊

Jokes aside, whether it takes the form of a 21st-century smart device or a common notebook and pen, the diary is something that can bridge the gap between the awareness of your intelligence and its mobilisation towards your intentions.

The diary, used as a tool, simply allows you to become more present to what's required of you and the process of its achievement.

However, if the diary alone were the answer, anyone who had one would be extremely successful, but this is not the case. Your diary has to be structured as a schematic of intelligence that will allow you to interpret your goals. You need to be working with your diary every day, ensuring that you are focusing on the following areas as minimum criteria:

INTELLECTUAL MAVERICK

Data collection	✔	**Evaluation tools**	✔	**Speculating**	✔
Measurement	✔	**Nature of the risk**	✔	**Hold yourself Accountable**	✔
Mapping your goal dependencies and your goal hierarchies	✔	**Creation of new opportunities**	✔	**Self-Management**	✔
Forecasting	✔	**Engineering strategies**	✔	**Strength of Execution**	✔

These points that we referred to will be expanded upon in the following chapters, and *The Jetstream* challenge is for you to read with a definite intent to identify the intellectual dynamics needed to engineer your greatest successes.

The success you achieve in life will become directly relative to the initiative, intelligence, and commitment that you apply to life, and a diary should serve as your tool in this regard.

INTELLECTUAL MAVERICK

Getting schooled in the process of using your diary correctly, over a lifetime, is what will allow you to have greater access to the blueprint of your consciousness. It brings immense structure, awareness and mindful intelligence that will, over a lifetime, add inconceivable value.

ENGINEER
CHANGE

Life requires more than a whisper of wisdom. Life actually requires the use of a diary, and when used correctly, your entries will reveal the following formula:

PROCESSING POWER × STRENGTH OF EXECUTION = THE JETSTREAM OF SUCCESS

Engineer change through the exhilaration of possibility.

DON'T BE
OVER-CONFIDENT
& DON'T BE
WEAK

YOUR
PROGRESS
LIES
IN THE
BALANCE

Rio Carnival

Rio Carnival
Undress your beliefs

INTELLECTUAL MAVERICK

Rio de Janeiro. The mere mention of the city causes your mind to erupt with thoughts of music, dancing and festivities. So... we jetted across the Atlantic to Rio de Janeiro, to participate in the lively, rhythmical native Brazilian dance, the samba, which is witnessed by millions of people annually.

The night is sultry and alive. As we arrive at the Samba-drome, the indecent excitement is positively magnetic. The grandstands are filled to capacity. The amazing spirit of magic is in the air;

THE MAGIC OF LOVE,

THE MAGIC OF CELEBRATION

& THE MAGIC OF CREATIVITY.

17:20:11 23
TO YOUR PODIUM FINISH

INTELLECTUAL MAVERICK

Two exotic women appear; my expression, one of utmost attention. Their goddess-like bodies glitter like gold. They are dressed in shimmering, embellished costumes that leave little to the imagination. My pulse quickens. The band breaks into drumbeats, and the women begin shimmying their hips. People go wild, shouting and cheering, urging them on. The faster the drums beat, the faster their hips move, and they begin dancing in a fierce and passionate manner as they make their way through.

AND SO THE CARNIVAL BEGINS...

an explosion of gold, scarlet, orange and yellow fills the Sambadrome as the first dance school makes its grand entrance with their float, a majestic lion, sitting proud with his golden mane. The crowd roars with excitement. Four thousand participants move as one, so precise is their timing. People all around dance the samba along with the performers. It seems to be the most natural movement and rhythm. Each float that follows seems to be more extravagant than the one before. The energy is electrifying. We are completely in awe as we watch the performers singing, dancing and parading to the signature of each float, which is framed around the rhythm of the music.

INTELLECTUAL MAVERICK

Our spirits soar *as we revel in* festivities.

Finally, we're next; our moment has arrived. The overwhelming feeling that blazed so unexpectedly inside us cause our hearts to pound madly. As we assume our positions, we are overcome with emotion.

UNDRESS YOUR BELIEFS

Even though we've been watching each school participate, nothing prepared us for what we were about to experience. It's our turn now. As we begin to dance, we feel more alive. It seems to awaken the dormant potential within us to new heights of expression.

We become fully immersed in the moment as we unleash the creativity from within us. It's almost as though we were able to redefine ourselves, elevating our beings to become one with the dance.

INTELLECTUAL
MAVERICK

Redefine YOURSELF

Factored into life:

Life is an expression, life is an experience, life is a celebration, a rhythm, an unfolding of magic. Shouldn't your beliefs be conducive to the qualities of life? The more life reveals to us, the less we know it, because the process of trying to know it, compounds its mystery.

WHAT ARE THE QUALITIES IN YOUR BELIEFS ?

Step out of your way!

We as a society undermine and de-value the positive and negative influences of beliefs. A belief is just a snapshot in time. Does it offer any value in isolation? Probably not, and if it does, then its contribution is very vague. The value is introduced in the relationship between your belief and your intention. This means that you have to have a very clear definition of the schematic of your intentions. We also need to take into account that life is in a constant progression, which means that your schematic should allow for this expansiveness.

This process sounds complex, but it simply means that you need to become the philosopher of your life. In context, a "philosopher" would be a person who would critically study the basic principles and concepts of subjects of his interest with the strength of awareness that would progressively engineer greater value.

DO YOUR BELIEFS CREATE **YOUR GOALS**

OR

ARE YOUR BELIEFS A RESULT OF ACHIEVING YOUR GOALS?

ARE YOU

WORTH MORE
THAN YOU
CAN EVER
IMAGINE

?

We engage ourselves directly relative to our aspirations and if you choose to be one of those outstanding individuals who aims for greatness, then your life's journey will constantly require you to push the boundaries to exceed the edge of reason and mobilise the required intelligence to achieve the miraculous. In this event, you will always find that your beliefs are a product of your aspirations. If you want to exhibit this quality, then you shouldn't stand rigidly wedded to what you believe in, but rather exceed your beliefs so that you can attain a state of mind that is conducive to your goal.

Your empowering beliefs give you a structured awareness to take action, and the adverse results you experience in your life are generally due to ill-defined areas of focus.

Now let's consider the business of your life; the success of which will be largely determined by your capacity to exceed your beliefs and to place your emphasis on the relationship between your belief and your intention.

INTELLECTUAL MAVERICK

UNDRESS YOUR BELIEFS

Become a Philosopher

INTELLECTUAL MAVERICK

To become the philosopher of your life is to develop an acute awareness of creating greater value. In order to achieve this, you need a frame of reference to create the resonance. The frame of reference here is going to be the composition of philosophies that you choose to employ to underpin your progress.

The philosophies that you choose will be a direct reflection of what you choose to achieve and your attitude towards life. You have to ask yourself, what does life require of you in terms of pushing the boundaries, while being deeply respectful at the same time?

WE NEED TO AWAKEN THE INTELLECTUAL MAVERICK WITHIN OURSELVES.

The following five philosophies form the framework of an intellectual maverick.

Irrevocably Change Your World

Piece together an ever-fuller understanding of yourself, with the intention of reinventing yourself a thousand fold. You should always aim towards exponential achievements, with the wisdom of knowing that you are not chasing the achievement, but rather chasing the consciousness of who you need to become in order to materialise your successes. You need to become the personification of success. Life is meant to be played as though it were a game. Be sure to swing for the fences.

Think with Sophistication

Sophisticated thinking is based on the conscious focus of your thoughts. Sophisticated thinkers are not really interested in a single decision or isolated decisions; they are however, interested in the process of making successful decisions over a lifetime. Essentially, we should never focus on a goal, but rather place all of our focus on the process of achieving that goal. Thinking within an intellectual paradigm and steering away from making emotional decisions are the qualities that will bring in a coherence and dynamism into our achievements.

Exceed Probability Amplitudes

Achieving success is your ability to eliminate the weaknesses and biases that are inherent within yourself. History tells us that not all greats have off-the-chart IQs, nor are they born with limitless freedom. In fact, it is this triumph over less than favourable circumstances and their determination to achieve that we tend to respect the most. The people who have changed the world are people like you and I. They set out to achieve outstanding results and make their decisions within intellectual criteria. All the greats have engaged a higher impulse, a higher bandwidth, and an inherent strength. What I'm actually referring to is for you to develop an intrinsic strength in your awareness. We have to create a synergy between our awareness and our subjects of interest. While being schooled in this process you will find that life will unveil itself like a tapestry of magic.

Smile with Radiance

Life is beauty in every direction, but we are unable to access or see it if we are too consumed with our lives and psychology. The simple truth is that you can only touch more of the beauty of life by touching your own beauty. If you look through the lens of love, gratitude and contribution, then you will be able to see and touch more of the infinite beauty that makes life on earth a heaven. Learn to smile like sunshine every day and brighten up your world.

Get Lucky

I would love to tell you that your destiny is written in the stars, but it is actually written within the confines of your interpretation. Luck has more to do with self-engagement than any random twist of fate. Be bold

INTELLECTUAL MAVERICK

UNDRESS YOUR BELIEFS

and champion your life to exceed the probability amplitude of any statistic of luck.

INTELLECTUAL MAVERICK

As you can see, if you were to evaluate the essence of what is being discussed, it adds to the life, direction and dimension of your beliefs. **A belief is an insight into a given subject in a shape that defines interpretation.**

Your philosophies will be the thread of psychological influence. They serve as a compelling force that facilitates your intentions, and allows you to avoid tendencies to fall victim to disempowering beliefs.

These five philosophies are just an initial framework. You need to take the time to nominate a vast composition of philosophies that are most conducive to your life. You need to engineer your life through the exhilaration of possibility. When you break out of your disempowering beliefs, and realise that you are simply a world of potential, more specifically, unlimited potential, then you will see life as the majestic experience that it truly is.

We need to become sophisticated in terms of defining what life requires of us. Your success is going to be a reflection of your commitment, creativity, boldness, wisdom, compassion, investigative skills, patience, aptitude and capacity to reinvent yourself.

Intelligence is knowing what's required of you,

so you need to define the qualities that are most conducive to your progress and then most importantly challenge your beliefs to decipher the greatest value so that it can be factored into your process to plan and achieve success.

We need to realise that our beliefs become our ideas and our ideas become the essence of our lives. Wise men say that wisdom is the realisation that we know virtually nothing, which simply means that when we realise that we know virtually nothing, that is when we are truly open to learn.

INTELLECTUAL MAVERICK

UNDRESS YOUR BELIEFS

We need to develop our capacity to evaluate more intently and get in tune with the rhythm of life.

INTELLECTUAL MAVERICK

The analogy of introducing the samba into your beliefs was intended to awaken lively and exotic qualities in them; to open an array of possibilities. Your beliefs should be a process of discovery that makes you feel alive. Super achievers seem to dance through life. They choreograph their beliefs with a passion and elegance that frames their successes.

We need to dance with a rhythm and flexibility that awakens a vibrancy and passion within the impulse of our being. Usher your presence into your beliefs and become an expression of life, captivated by possibility and one with your beliefs of supremacy. You are worth more than you can ever imagine.

The genius creates himself.

Line of Sight

Line of Sight
Instinct is the gap between thought and emotion

INTELLECTUAL MAVERICK

Finally, the much-anticipated; mystical, ethnic-styled envelope arrived. Black, roped with twine, decorated with feathers and African beads, it evoked in us a child-like sense of embarking upon a treasure hunt. We had been invited, along with five other couples, to join billionaire Sir Richard Branson and his wife, Joan, for a weekend at their private game reserve, Ulusaba.

Ulusaba, meaning "place of little fear", was aptly named to remind us of the native warriors who stood guard on a mountaintop here hundreds of years ago, alerting their tribe of potential danger or enemies. Ironically, as we jet away from the city to this "place of little fear", and as we fly over the vast expanse of untouched beauty and untamed beasts, we can't help but feel an uncontrollable sense of fear gripping us.

DEVELOP YOUR INSTINCT

14:47:36 53
TO YOUR PODIUM FINISH

INTELLECTUAL
MAVERICK

We set foot on the hot, sandy runway, hearts beating faster and harder till they seemed to beat as one with the tribal drums that welcomed us.

Smiling Africans raise a cloud of crimson dust with their rhythmical barefoot dancing. Their high-pitched songs of joy resonate within our very soul. I gaze at faces filled with delight and pride as we connect as one. Throughout this warm welcome we can't help wondering whether we are being watched. Periodically, we dart precautionary glances towards the bushes nearby in a feeble attempt to be one step ahead of a predator, for this is the land where the Big Five roam freely against the sun-drenched primal African landscape. One can't help but feel a sense of belonging in Africa, a sense of origin, as though we are at the very heart of the world.

After a glass of much-needed crisp champagne, we are each equipped with a pair of binoculars and safari gear. We get into our open-topped Land Rovers and drive to the lodges. They are built on stilts and nestled on the mountaintop overlooking the reserve, yet unprotected. We had to be escorted from our rooms to any other part of the lodge by an armed game ranger. There are no taking chances.

Sir Richard Branson, myself and Mike Higgins, at Ulusaba.

Our five-thirty a.m. game drive is an eventful one. Apart from the fact that Sir Richard Branson is driving our four-by-four, we have the rare opportunity of seeing a kudu in the middle of the river surrounded by four crocodiles. Its urgent and desperate cry for help resounds through the denseness of the reserve. We watch in anticipation; a three-ton hippo arrives on the scene. She seems desperate to protect the kudu, and chases the crocs off in the opposite direction.

As we head back, one of the highlights of the trip begins to unfold. The rangers signal each other, engines are turned off; there's a deafening silence.

INTELLECTUAL MAVERICK

INTELLECTUAL MAVERICK

Within range is one of the most awesome creatures I've ever seen - a leopard preparing to attack his prey. His luxurious coat is in absolute harmony with his surroundings. Although he senses his audience, he doesn't lose focus on the lone buck grazing nearby. The buck looks up with a fearful glance, sensing the danger that shadows ahead. The leopard waits patiently, calculating every move with a remarkable precision, stealthily moving each time the buck moves. He begins to move slowly towards it, every muscle flexed with a definite purpose.

An icy chill
— sweeps over the audience

as each person silently decides whose side they are on; predator or prey. The leopard's speed is instantaneous, its paws barely touching the ground. At the same moment the buck instinctively springs into action, its graceful body darting through the grass.

The leopard responds with a defiant speed. The buck senses the leopard closing in, gains energy and quickens its spring.

The *race* is a fierce **struggle** between **predator** and prey,

INTELLECTUAL MAVERICK

each one moving through the air in leaps. The seconds pass in a prolonged and painful silence. The buck begins to show fatigue, losing momentum as it makes a final struggle to get away. Its efforts are in vain; it makes the fatal mistake of showing signs of defeat, which triggers a sense of victory in the leopard. Four quick strides and the predator makes its final powerful leap. It's all over in a moment.

DEVELOP YOUR INSTINCT

BECOME THE INSTRUMENT OF YOUR INTENTION

INSTINCTIVELY FINDING YOUR LINE OF SIGHT

To achieve success is to establish and execute key principles that are conducive to the results you seek. We are meant to employ each day as a stride towards our achievements. We need to rediscover our willpower and inherent strength so as to awaken the greatness that is the natural order of our soul. Developing this mental competitive edge will help us to define the process of achieving our goals. This clarity and visibility is a function of intelligence. However, conjuring the picture of our past, present and future is more deceptive than we can recognise. It seems that we are perceptually misled by mental faculties that are inherent in us.

We all want to live a life where we love and are loved. We want to create moments and engineer possibility into greatness. However, we tend to discount the staggering number of thoughts we have each day, and as a result, become jaded in our capacity to see through a clear mind.

INTELLECTUAL MAVERICK

DEVELOP YOUR INSTINCT

We need to consider the influence of our proactive thinking and reactive thinking.

We have tens of thousands of thoughts per day.

Over 90% of the thoughts we have today are a repetition from yesterday, leaving us at a disadvantage in our endeavour to expand our lives.

We view life predominantly through the following lenses:

Ego mind: the state of mind where we see ourselves in context of social expectations. It's a fear-based mind that is constantly seeking favour.

Rational mind: the mind of deduction. It operates within the laws of probability, statistics and mathematics. It's the reasoning, analytical part of the mind. However, when we consider that we are a lifetime of potential, we realise that the creation of our future successes also become infinite and the rational mind, in context, often finds itself out of its depth.

Personal unconscious: This is the range of mind that's governed by our experiences and memories. It distorts our interpretation of reality. This mind in most individuals is more negatively inclined. As an example, if you were paid a compliment and an insult, you'd be more inclined to remember the insult.

If you are predominantly engaged in your ego mind, your rational mind and your personal unconscious, then, true success can only flow into your absence. These three minds distract us from our intentions to the extent that they lose their relevance and we are unable to decode the value of our intent and willpower to progress. Our everyday lives become a representation of a weak mental faculty as we imitate the mentalities of conflicting psychologies. The influence has far-reaching consequences because our outer world is a mirror of our inner world.

INTELLECTUAL MAVERICK

DEVELOP YOUR INSTINCT

Finding your line of sight is about developing your instinct to direct your intellect and profound common sense.

In order for you to effectively leverage this awareness, let's venture into the domain of humour, so that it becomes more memorable.

INTELLECTUAL MAVERICK

If I were a leopard looking at my prey through the lens of my **EGO MIND**, what line of sight would I have? Again, my ego mind is where I see myself in context of social expectations. It's a fear-based mind that's constantly seeking favour.

If I as the leopard were looking through the lens of my ego, it would probably be telling me something like, what would my friends think of me if I didn't get the buck? Or even worse, what would the buck think of me? I can just imagine him exaggerating the story of how he outran a leopard. I'm really getting tired of fast food.

Or what if I run into a pack of hyenas? I can picture them rolling on their backs, hysterical with laughter.

I'm not getting any younger, **my *spots* are getting** *lighter*, **and I'm standing around** talking to myself.

If I looked at my prey through my **RATIONAL MIND**, then it would probably say to me, I'm not as fast as I used to be. Besides, look at that mountainous terrain. It's only going to slow me down, and this buck has his youth going for him. What chance do I have? He's probably just going to jog away from me. I still have to go through a selection process. If I don't catch it, what is the alternative supply of prey in the area relative to my demands? My rational mind would probably make me consider risk factors as well, for example, what is the probability of my tripping over an uprooted tree? What if I get hurt by some unforeseen circumstance?

And finally, if I looked through the lens of my

PERSONAL UNCONSCIOUS,

my memory would be more inclined to remind me of all my failed attempts, hurts, and the range in my temperaments over the years.

I'm sure you get the idea.

INTELLECTUAL
MAVERICK

If I were the leopard and viewed my prey through these three lenses, I would be highly unlikely to survive on my own. I would probably have to set up camp with the vultures.

Let's consider the actual leopard in the story. What lens do you think he was looking through in order to execute his intention with such determination, precision and speed? Undoubtedly, he was looking through the lens of his instinct. He instinctively found his line of sight.

Become the instrument of your intention.

It seems that we as a society tend to take life too seriously. The great seers and high priests suggest that life in its highest and simplest interpretation is just a game. It is meant to test us as part of our evolutionary progress. I have learned through my challenges and victories that if you think you are playing the game, then the game is probably playing you. How do we crack the coded sequence that choreographs life's stillness and wonder, its richness and illusions? Life is meant to be a demonstration of acumen, human touch, intuitive processes, silence and synchronistic self-engagement as a minimum. Although all these processes run independently, they are all richly interrelated. The insight required to manage their interrelatedness is a process of self-mastery.

I would be understating if I said it is as difficult as trying to look into a fully lit mirror in full view of your reflection, yet not seeing yourself.

INTELLECTUAL MAVERICK

DEVELOP YOUR INSTINCT

INTELLECTUAL
MAVERICK

The reflection of your ego mind, rational mind and personal unconscious is so evident that it's almost incomprehensible to dismiss. The outer world is just a mirror of you. We've been conditioned to think that we attract what we desire, but the reality is, we don't attract what we desire, we attract who we are. Investigating the **corridors** of **time** is what will allow us to see what qualities we are demonstrating mentally, emotionally and spiritually. We need to realise that we are actually investing ourselves into the bank of time and the return on investment is directly relative.

We have to recognise that our intentions have an internal environment. It is for this reason that we need to place our emphasis on having consciousness goals. To achieve success we need to become the instruments of our intentions, so that we can engineer them to be more conducive to the results we seek.

THE GENIUS CREATES HIMSELF.

An intention is both a product and a process. We need to define what's required of us. Become that person and factor yourself into life.

Life requires us to always have focused intentions. Opportunities are always present, but the turbulence created by our ego mind, rational mind and personal unconscious will hinder us from identifying them. We must strive to instinctively find our line of sight from moment to moment. In the case of the leopard, each stride counts. In our case, it is every passing day that counts.

The outer world is a consequence of the inner world, and those who pay close attention and become educated in this relationship will progress the quickest. Life requires us to step it up when it counts. We need to demonstrate the mental sharpness to design and implement our plans of action while allocating our resources effectively.

INTELLECTUAL MAVERICK

DEVELOP YOUR INSTINCT

INTELLECTUAL
MAVERICK

ENGINEER
POSSIBILITY
INTO
GREATNESS.

Line of Sight was written to help you develop your instinct, which in context is the natural impulse used to recognise the attributes required for successful performance.

We need to place great emphasis on our comprehensive needs and be very meditative in the way we develop our instinct to achieve them. Our disciplined focus will help us overcome our need to imitate weak mental faculties.

Instinctive successful behaviour is responding within intellectual frameworks and sequences to achieve clearly defined goals. This is a mental faculty that has to be defined and developed so that we can leverage our days with greater self-engagement.

We need to become instinctively sensitive to intelligent action as a natural tendency to develop a greater coherence within our mind, body and spirit. We need to be progressively and consistently awakened to our natural impulse to react intelligently. The development of this instinct will allow us to journey into the magic and mystery of our true potential, creativity and strength. It will take us beyond our intellect and create our luck like a tapestry of magic.

Success
is a definition.

We need to define the miraculous and awaken the instinct that is conducive to our greatness.

INTELLECTUAL MAVERICK

DEVELOP YOUR INSTINCT

COMMIT TO A LIFE OF ACHIEVEMENT.

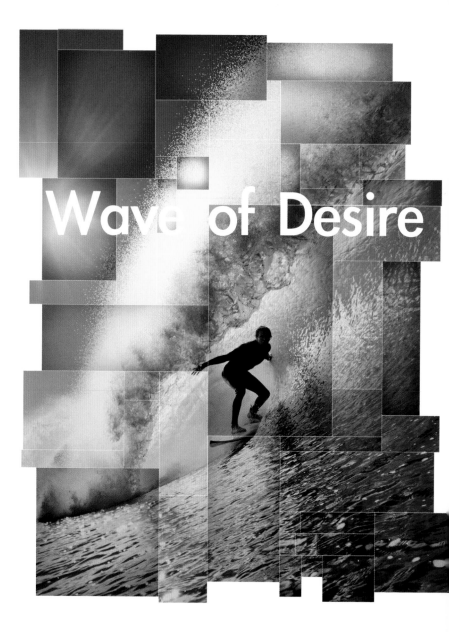

Wave of Desire
Surf through your sacredness

INTELLECTUAL MAVERICK

I begin to stir up my signature dish, Szechuan prawn, prepared with a red sauce rich in ginger, garlic and pepper. The bottle of choice wine is opened. South African vineyards are cradled in-between lush valleys and mountain ranges where man and nature conspire to create some of the most renowned wines world-wide. Its aroma reveals an unknown era in time.

I step out onto my balcony and before me is an un-mistakable vision of beauty: the Indian Ocean. With each glance at the ocean I am filled with a familiar sense of wonder. I watch the waves as they rise like colossal beings; the ocean glistening in the sunlight. My spirit is elevated yet humbled with a deep appreciation and, in case you are wondering, it certainly is not the effect of the wine.

11:28:47²⁴
TO YOUR PODIUM FINISH

INTELLECTUAL
MAVERICK

Time flies by as our group of friends indulge in witty humour. Then finally, knowing its time and place, the tide comes in, boldly challenging us to take it on. With panther-like strides, we make our way across the soft sand, passing a flock of birds inquisitively searching for their next meal. Then, we break into a run, clutching onto our surfboards as we dive eagerly into the exhilarating ocean. The water is invigorating after a day in the African sun. As I paddle further out, I see a variety of shoaling fish glistening in the sunlight.

I go further in, I can feel the primordial power and energy of each new wave. Civilisation fades away with the intensity, the life and the emotion of every new wave; each one offering a revived opportunity for a challenge. Each new wave comes rising rapidly with enormous speed, with an upsurge of energy more exuberant and powerful than the previous one. It's a whole new world, generated by power and energy.

YOUR

ABSOLUTE

TRIUMPH.

INTELLECTUAL MAVERICK

Within each one of us lie oceans of potential, oceans of capacity and oceans of aspiration. The energy that causes these glassy oceans within us to rise up to waves of power, breaking all known boundaries, is the element of a great flame of desire. Our spirits, intelligence and creativity are crystallised in value by our desire.

LIVE FROM THE HEART

Factored into life:

INTELLECTUAL MAVERICK

The word value in terms of self-worth suggests such profound contrast between successful and unsuccessful societies. The truth is, there is a segment of society that has become hugely successful who were not born with skills, talent and the capacity to be sophisticated thinkers. These are traits that they made a conscious effort to seek and acquire, to serve them in their quest to be extravagant in their self-engagement.

IMMENSE SELF-MADE WEALTH IS EVIDENCE OF A GRANDLY RICH MIND.

If you were to strip a self-made immensely rich person of all his possessions, it would just be a matter of time before he amasses his wealth again. Should he choose, he could probably acquire it in a fraction of the time and with greater ease than before, now having the advantage of hindsight. The success we are referring to is not limited to monetary success; the same rules apply in all aspects of success. We are all endowed with the innate traits to become super achievers in life, provided we awaken to the realisation that our process of achievement always starts inwardly first, and then expresses itself outwardly.

Success requires us to be more result-orientated, decisive, conclusive, influential, resourceful, and exhibit a keen desire to progress. However, there is a factor that diminishes our capabilities and that is what I call *self-inflicted sabotage.* We sabotage ourselves when we fail to recognise that we are exhibiting disempowering qualities.

INTELLECTUAL MAVERICK

LIVE FROM THE HEART

Any form of sadness, agitation, emotional fatigue, sense of being unfavourably overwhelmed, or having an over-controlling nature, diminishes our capacity to be consistently purposeful.

This *self-inflicted sabotage* is even more damaging when we justify and give in to these disempowering qualities. Our repeated excuse for falling victim to this sabotage is framed in our efforts to cope with life. In doing that, we don't realise how much it affects our brain chemistry, our hormones, our mental and physical well-being.

Our supposed efforts to cope are what dilutes our attention from where it really needs to be. Super achievers realise that their life oscillates between two demands: The first is the need to cope, and the second is that of accountability of intelligence and action.

I could be wrong, but to me, it seems as though we develop this need to cope from our early schooling years, where the quantum of information always seemed to surpass our level of maturity. That made us feel there was always something more we had to learn, to know, to master, in order to survive academically. That level of expectation remains in our awareness as we become career-orientated, however, the word coping is generally associated with a strained effort, which is often the result of insufficient intelligence in our process of achieving.

The turning point with any super achiever was probably when they made the conscious choice to orientate their lives towards accountability of intelligence and action. They acknowledge the responsibility to quantify intelligent actions. They would have held themselves answerable to progress.

WE NEED TO

SELF-EVALUATE

BECAUSE ACCOUNTABILITY IS A DIRECT

REFLECTION

OF OUR LEVELS OF DESIRE.

INTELLECTUAL MAVERICK

Let's go through a simple exercise:

INTELLECTUAL
MAVERICK

If I said the word, "love",
what three words come to mind?

-

-

-

If I said the word, "career",
what three words come to mind?

-

-

-

If I said the word, "intelligence",
what three words come to mind?

-

-

-

If I said the word, "exercise",
what three words come to mind?

-

-

-

The words that you have chosen to associate with these four subjects speak nothing of the subject, but they do however speak volumes of you as a person. These words are a direct reflection of your current accountability pertaining to these four subjects.

SUPER ACHIEVERS
TAKE CONSISTENT ACTION THAT IS
DISCIPLINED,
INTELLIGENT
AND FOCUSED.

INTELLECTUAL MAVERICK

Their demands, willpower, ambitious nature and general personality traits are conducive to them achieving their goals.

Super achievers almost seem to stand on a surfboard of time. They align themselves with time as they discover, manoeuvre and play with the rhythm of each wave, each emotion. They seemingly school themselves in an awareness that expands their repertoire, and improves their technique of surfing through their life's experiences.

Super achievers are those who have taught themselves to jump from one reality to another. That leap is everything; IT'S WHERE THEIR GENIUS LIES. They cross this threshold of monumental self-discovery. They stand on the surfboard of time and manoeuvre the expression of their souls, their desires, their transcendence of thinking and feeling into miraculous achievements. They seem to understand that the more they awaken their greater soul, the greater the experience of life will be revealed.

INTELLECTUAL MAVERICK

How do they transcend their thinking and feeling to the portal that awakens possibility?

We all have those powers and abilities. It's the natural order of our soul. This chapter, *Wave of Desire*, was written to help you engage your soul, and I plan on doing this by positioning you on the surfboard of time.

You've got to know which waves to go after, and which waves to let pass. You definitely want to avoid jealousy, anger, envy and anything else detrimental. Those are the type of waves that can knock you over in a way that can virtually cripple your progress.

The ever-changing waves of emotions demand unwavering balance, stance, and rhythm to achieve optimisation of life.

Riding the wave of your desire should be:

1. An emotional awareness.

2. A progression toward the crystallisation of your desire.

3. The tool that enhances your spiritual advantage.

INTELLECTUAL MAVERICK

LIVE FROM THE HEART

INTELLECTUAL
MAVERICK

Living successfully is maintaining an awareness of conscious focus; it's exercising your powers of self-influence. It's your capacity to manoeuvre through the shape, structure, dimension, life and direction of your progress. It's bringing different elements of a multi-faceted awareness into a relationship that gives you greater efficiency.

There are several ways of doing this, but I personally use the following declarations as a way of achieving meditative awareness to reinvent myself and make every moment count. These five points are meant to serve as a platform to open the gateway to exploration.

STEP 1: THE SIMPLE LAW OF THE UNIVERSE IS THAT YOU CREATE YOUR OWN REALITY.

If you say this declaration once, it will stimulate your thought. If you say it ten times out loud with the right emotion, it will summon your strength. If you say it a million times like I have, through life's challenges and victories, then I assure you that these words will irrevocably change your world. Not only will you have a stance and position of strength, you will realise your potential to act. It will take your mind and your instinct to a whole new dimension.

STEP 2: ELEVATE YOUR STANDARDS.

Create a written commitment defining your miraculous achievements in a variety of areas in your life. The more comprehensively definitive the definitions, the greater the achievements will be. Define everything starting from health, love, contribution, and all of your aspirations that will facilitate your evolution.

INTELLECTUAL MAVERICK

LIVE FROM THE HEART

STEP 3: LIVE FROM THE HEART.

INTELLECTUAL
MAVERICK

SUPER ACHIEVERS
ARE THOSE WHO HAVE
HEART.

What is heart?

Heart is a place of interpretation that defines who you are and who you become. This is your return to innocence. It's a place where you can't judge yourself with rigid criteria. This is most important to unleash your potential. Remember that to free the mind awakens the heart. When was the last time you lived from the heart?

STEP 4: LIVE ON THE EDGE OF WHAT IS POSSIBLE, FOR WITHIN ME IS THE SEED OF GREATNESS.

Use this as a declaration to awaken your greater spirit, and invite the spirit of adventure. It's meant to elevate your thinking and feeling to take you to the threshold of employing your genius.

INTELLECTUAL MAVERICK

STEP 5: I AWAKEN THE GREATEST FLAME OF DESIRE.

This is the most important declaration, as it evolves your criteria towards the crystallisation of your superhuman qualities. Super achievers exhibit superhuman qualities, and every one of those qualities are innate in us all.

There's an obvious threshold to open the gateway of achievement, and that hinges on the structural framework of your desire.

LIVE FROM THE HEART

INTELLECTUAL MAVERICK

Imagine expressing and exercising a degree of desire like Bill Gates, Steven Spielberg, Mother Teresa or Barack Obama. What makes them extraordinary is their psychology; the way they view the world influences who they are and who they become. Life seems to play out within a sequence of events in an all-encompassing coherent framework. It's mind-blowing to consider the ambiguous threads that lavishly interlace these patterns.

I define life as

experience.

It's nothing more, nothing less. It just simply is. To acutely illuminate the mystery that sanctions and frees these experiences is a process of recognition and this awareness will reveal life's purest marvel.

The Jetstream of Success was designed to alter the very essence of your perception and open the gateway for exploration, so prepare yourself to journey into the recognition of your sacredness.

Are you ready?
Okay, let's do it.

Our souls come from eternity, and go to eternity. Desire is the actual journey through your sacredness. It's you traveling into and through the concealed composition of your psychology. Desire is psychology, because it is the transcendence of thinking and feeling.

To touch your sacredness is a process of awakening the heart and freeing the mind, which leads you to a place called the soul. To know the soul - now that's a cool thought. To touch your soul through your humanity is the ultimate expression of a great flame of desire. The flame of your soul, which blazes your total to life, is desire.

Imagine travelling to a place where you are consumed by your desire, and without the desire you find yourself wanting; a constant exploration that empowers you into the continuum of your potentiality.

INTELLECTUAL MAVERICK

Hey, come on, take a deep breath.

Relax, pay attention to the rhythm and depth of your breath. Imagine everything you are and everything that you will be is in that breath. Shouldn't we be inspired by that breath? I wonder what it means to be inspired.

Inspiration is in the **unknown.**

What's the last thing you learned about yourself? Mmmm, interesting. There is nothing more elusive than the obvious. It means you are most elusive to yourself.

Is desire the magnificence of your innocence, or is it the process of reflecting life back to itself? Like a magician, your existence is in time and you reflect the expression of time back into time, a constant process of orchestrating time like a symphony of magic defining experience.

INTELLECTUAL MAVERICK

DESIRE

Your desire is your life force. It's your stimulating spark in the process of transmutation. Desire is the starting point of an ever-evolving awareness. It's the recognition that brings you to the presence of a challenge. Desire mobilises action to move towards your intention. It takes you beyond the paradigm of a defeatist attitude and it permeates every facet of your intentions. Desire is the reason we strive. Your desire excels and amplifies you.

INTELLECTUAL MAVERICK

The greatest flame of desire is what awakens your superhuman qualities. Success is a product of desire. Desire is the journey in your evolutionary path that is meant to serve you. Desire is the element that accelerates success, facilitating one expression of life to another. It's a spectrum that needs to be integrated to the full.

LIVE FROM THE HEART

IT'S NOT WHERE YOU ARE, IT'S WHO YOU ARE, AND KNOWING THAT THE FUTURE IS IN THE PALM OF YOUR HAND.

INTELLECTUAL TALENT WILL GIVE US AN UPPER-HAND IN THE GAME OF LIFE.

FORTUNATELY, WE ALL CAN DEVELOP IT.

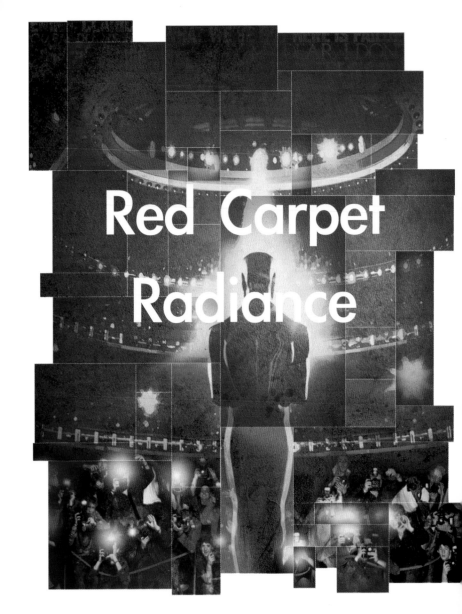

Red Carpet Radiance

Red Carpet Radiance
You are on the stage of life

It's Oscar Night; a crisp, cool evening as everyone prepares for the most anticipated movie industry event of the year. The exhilaration is overwhelming as thousands of stargazers anticipate the arrival of their favourite celebrities. Camera crews standing by eagerly, waiting to capture the numerous arriving stars. The event is televised on virtually every entertainment channel worldwide. Fans tune in as the curiosity builds up to the fashion spectacle. Fashion designers are waiting with baited breath, hoping their garments will be chosen. An explosion of emotions sweeps over the crowd as each star steps out of their limousine to the reverence of their fans and onto the red carpet. The men, dashing in their tailored tuxedos; the women, breathtaking in the most elaborate designer gowns imaginable, adorning flawless diamonds and radiant smiles.

INTELLECTUAL MAVERICK

YOUR STAR QUALITY

08:03:31:01
TO YOUR PODIUM FINISH

INTELLECTUAL
MAVERICK

Months of planning and preparation now culminate in the start of the most anticipated evening in show business. A celebration of achievements in the arena of entertainment ignites the night.

You're Invited

YOU'RE STANDING ON THE RED CARPET.

Allow me the honour of escorting you.

"Trust me, it will be a breeze,"

I'll whisper the moment.

"Slowly, turn around and smile, it's your time."

"Now brace yourself, Julia Roberts is walking towards you." Her smile can only be described as absolute sunshine.

"Ok, relax; reaffirm your poise. Elegance and charm are the order of the day. Centre yourself; a heightened degree of self-awareness can only be found in stillness. Look over your shoulder; is that Brad Pitt?" Now let's be honest, who wouldn't want to exude that level of sex appeal?

INTELLECTUAL MAVERICK

YOUR STAR QUALITY

Later on, "Did you just brush George Clooney's arm or was that his distinguished charm? Celebrate the moment; revel in the glory. Smile; life is a simple magic."

"Wait, listen, is that Cameron Diaz's infectious laugh?"

Flash! A camera startles you. Okay, gently turn around. I want you to meet someone.

Have you ever met someone who completely blew your mind with their radiance, elegance and captivating presence? Someone who naturally commanded authority?

This is where I venture into the domain where I introduce you to *yourself.*

INTELLECTUAL
MAVERICK

Your Star *Quality*

INTELLECTUAL MAVERICK

Take a deep breath.

You are outstanding, radiant and confident.

You are revealing an attractiveness that's overwhelmingly magnetic.

The crowd is mesmerised by your whisper of sensuality.

You are truly desirable, cheerful and playful.

You have a spring in your step and you are glowing with a pure, fresh, radiant energy.

You are absolute sunshine, and you are exuding the warmth of its life-force.

Your creativity is shining through every given moment.

You have discovered your brilliance and rhythm with this moment.

You are living in the intoxicating experience where everything is possible. Your body seems to be speaking a language of love and your spirit is elevated to a point where the magic of your persona is revealed.

You are intoxicated in love with the moment and you are the height of admiration.

The best of you is pulsating into the life of the moment.

You are awakened to the realisation that the mind is the most extraordinary asset in creation.

Your presence is exhibiting an energy that embraces just about everyone that is present.

You were born to *stand out.*

"Hi, I'm Julian."
"It's an honour to meet you!"

We are on the *stage of life* every day, and you are the *star* of the show.

YOUR STAR QUALITY

All the stars that find themselves on the red carpet have not just arrived there by sheer luck. These are individuals who have learned at some point to awaken and express their star quality, and they, just like us, have been on a quest to be something more. They have faced their challenges, their heartbreaks and setbacks, and still they persevere. To awaken our star quality, we need to be on a journey to be the best that we can be. We know the climb to our aspirations is vertical, but we don't have the luxury of giving up.

INTELLECTUAL
MAVERICK

We have reached this point in our lives. We've invested a lifetime, and the one thing that we've learned is that we will not settle for less than greatness.

Red Carpet Radiance is really a type of spiritual elegance, and the greatness we speak of is the whisper of charm that creates your radiance. Awakening your star quality is a schooling of your expressiveness.

Every second, we speak a language without using words;

a non-verbal language, and this language reveals more of us than we might care to reveal. It is more powerful than words and, once mastered, this tool can be applied in your favour to awaken a greater degree of intrigue. Actors are constantly investing a spectrum of energy into the scene. We are also exhibiting a spectrum of energy from moment to moment. Consider what energy we are consistently investing into our lives - whether it's a smile, a kiss, a thank you, a suggestion or any other component of interaction. We should be exhibiting a greater range in our energy.

Now, let's consider for a moment the art of acting.

Consider the instruments that an actor needs to employ in creating an extraordinary performance. His entire being, his body, mind, spirit, emotions, voice; these are his instruments. Actors need to master the use of these instruments in their full capacity. They need to intentionally strive for a heightened degree of self-awareness.

When your mind is disciplined to be aware of your intentions for long enough, then your coherence becomes stronger, and the manner in which you mindfully engage yourself becomes instinctive. An actor's mind is disciplined to constantly realign itself with the intention of a focused performance.

To become a star is within one's ability to achieve; all that is required is the knowledge and awareness of the inner dynamics of the role in order to deliver an intense and captivating performance.

INTELLECTUAL MAVERICK

YOUR STAR QUALITY

Legendary actors know how to transform themselves completely into their roles; and thus an actor's entire being is his instrument.

INTELLECTUAL MAVERICK

We need to

shine

through

—————————————————— life.——

When we look at the mystic art of alchemy, we venture into the possibility of shaping, changing and transmuting our realities. The outer world is a mirrored projection of our inner world.

To awaken your star quality is to find the centre of yourself; as opposed to being self-centred. Your radiant heart, being, mind, body, and spirit, with their surroundings will constitute your star quality.

To live successfully, you need to ensure that all of these elements are brought into a harmony and equilibrium.

In our daily lives, our star quality becomes diminished and undermined by any thoughts that are destructive or hurtful, be it toward a single person or humanity at large. This mental state severely dulls your star quality, and it's not possible for you to shine in these moments.

We need to strive for *happiness.*

We've all heard **gurus and high seers define happiness as a state of being.** They describe it almost as some opulent silence that's almost inconceivably elusive to achieve. In true *Jetstream* style, happiness is not that difficult to attain.

The reality is, we don't live in isolation. We live in a world of about seven billion people. Happiness is the art of giving and receiving.

INTELLECTUAL MAVERICK

YOUR STAR QUALITY

However, in most societies, many individuals want to receive happiness or radiance without giving. This one-sided approach places us in disharmony and less able to receive life's majestic promises.

We all sometimes fall victim to our poor demeanour, bad attitude and self-righteousness. What we don't realise is that we are building a divide that separates us from our grandeur as effectively as the Berlin Wall separated the East from the West.

I don't know if it's obvious to you or not, but it seems that we build this wall of ours with the following characteristics:

Attitude of Superiority

When we try to stand on a pedestal daily, then we isolate ourselves from humanity. We dress this attitude up with "that's who I am, those are the values I have" and so on. The reality is, we are cultivating an attitude of wanting to be served rather than to serve. Again, this goes against the art of giving and receiving and it dulls your radiance.

Pride

Your pride is directly relative to your level of maturity. It's generally associated with an inferiority complex. We should never be proud of our achievements, rather be thankful for them. Pride is associated with arrogance and ego. These qualities just diminish the magic of life. The magic of you is awakened by a grateful attitude and a willingness to share in your glory and celebrations of achievements.

Malicious Thoughts

All thoughts and emotions are always self-inflicted first. It's impossible not to resent yourself when harbouring resentful thoughts towards another. It's just an ugly place to be. The sooner you make the choice to just let them go, whether you are justified in having them or not, the sooner you'll be on your

INTELLECTUAL MAVERICK

synchronistic path to success. Bear in mind that you don't really recoup a loss if you lose inner strength in the process. Harbouring resentment doesn't gain you anything – in fact you lose equanimity and serenity with any form of resentment.

I have just given you a few examples of how we dull our radiance. Now, you need to take the initiative to define and evaluate for yourself all of your qualities that block your radiance from falling on the face of everyone you interact with. There is an upside to this; in the same fashion that a self-inflicted misery of mind multiplies itself a thousand-fold, the purpose of *Red Carpet Radiance* is meant to take you forward exponentially into your star quality so that your smile can shine brighter on your authentic path to happiness. You have got to become aware of the vast scope of energy within you and place your emphasis on awakening your star quality as a daily practice.

Your synergy with life and your progressive happiness will be largely determined by the way you structure your radiant heart, being, mind, body, and spirit, with their surroundings. Strive to be in harmony with your progressive happiness, which simply equates to the art of giving and receiving.

You see, **everyone is endowed with the star quality.** We need to define the degree of wakefulness that will allow this radiance to become our natural state. We need to become a student of our own history and awaken those qualities, which will offer satisfaction, peace, harmony and richness in life that will facilitate our actions in ways that are far beyond comprehension.

All of these qualities are just an impulse of energy that can be developed, and the way to expedite its development is to love your mind. Your thoughts and radiance, factored into the art of giving and receiving should be the language of your world. Develop the qualities that you feel will be beneficial to you. Awaken them exponentially and share them.

INTELLECTUAL MAVERICK

YOUR STAR QUALITY

INTELLECTUAL MAVERICK

Use these qualities from moment to moment. Make them your lifestyle, act on them, because you are on the stage of life every day.

Now go on, take the stage. Remember that there are no rehearsals, and no second takes.

Give *life* your ultimate *performance.*

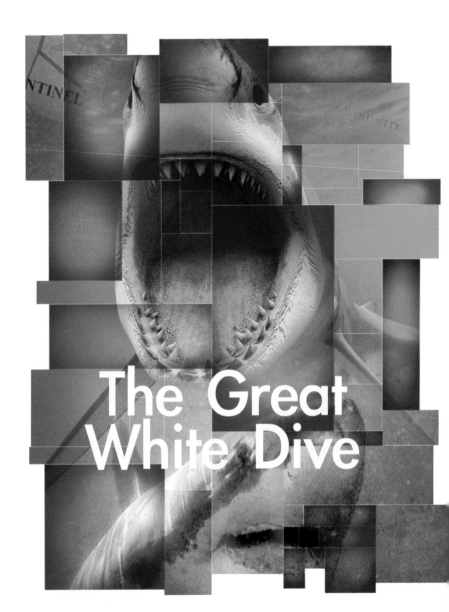

The Great
White Dive

The Great White Dive

Fear is just a message

"There is a creature alive today who has survived millions of years of evolution without change, without passion and without logic. It lives to kill. A mindless eating machine, it will attack and devour anything.

It is as though God created the devil and gave him JAWS."

From the preview of the 1975 motion picture *Jaws*.

Since viewing that movie as a child, I have had a compelling need to delve into the mysteries of this awesome predator. Decades later, I find myself researching before deciding to experience the Great White dive.

INTELLECTUAL MAVERICK

05:50:18 08
TO YOUR PODIUM FINISH

INTELLECTUAL MAVERICK

The Great White shark is an apex predator, which places it at the very top of its food chain. Its secret weapon in its arsenal of predation is its highly-developed sense of smell. It has the ability to detect the most minuscule amount of blood in the water - as little as one part in several million. It also has the ability to sense the electrical field generated even by the flexing of a single muscle. The primary attack strategy of a Great White is to bite a chunk off its prey, leaving it wounded or dead, and returning shortly thereafter to devour an easy meal. Imagine this; a 2.2 ton, 6 metre predator that can swim at speeds of up to 42 kilometres per hour.

The more time I spend researching the Great White, the more awakened I become to the spectrum of emotions within me. In spite of every instinct urging me not to pursue this venture, I had to meet this fearsome creature face to face. I decide to accept the challenge and take the plunge in Cape Town, South Africa. The month of May heralds the peak season for Great White activity off the coast of the "fairest Cape".

THE BIG DAY IS FINALLY HERE.

I'm indulging in a champagne breakfast in a restaurant at the water's edge of the Victoria & Alfred Waterfront mall. A smile dawns on my face as I observe a three-year-old boy eagerly try to nab a seagull perched on an aged wooden deck.

In the distance, I see the magnificent Table Mountain. The cloud cover, referred to as the "tablecloth", is cascading over the silhouette of the mountain. It seems to reveal the progressive beauty of being in the presence of a thousand angels. Anyone who has seen Table Mountain will testify of its soul-stirring majestic presence enveloping the city.

My phone rings, jolting me out of the moment. Knowing that it's the charter boat company, I'm almost reluctant to answer the call. I'm asked to go to Hout Bay, and from there, I'll take a helicopter to Gansbaai, where the boat departs on our expedition.

INTELLECTUAL MAVERICK

FEAR IS JUST A MESSAGE

As I drive, I instinctively begin viewing my surroundings as though it were for the very last time. I drive through Clifton and see houses with intriguing architecture nestled against bare rock faces. Further on in Camps Bay, the waves of the deep sapphire ocean breaking on the white sandy beaches, sets the stage for the glamourous to flaunt their latest Italian supercars and other extravagant indulgences. It's a trendy runway for jet-setters. On its main avenue, parallel to the beach, sidewalks are alive with the overflow from busy restaurants and cocktail bars.

Towering on my left are the Twelve Apostles, a mountain range with 12 distinct peaks which are likened to the 12 Apostles from Biblical scripture - are the Apostles desperately trying to convey a word of warning?

A typical evening view of Table Mountain, Cape Town.

I approach Hout Bay, and spot my sister Rozanne's home, nestled in dense forestry with one of the most spectacular views on earth. I was there just a few days ago, playing soccer with my niece Isabella. My mind echoes the word "remember". If the dive goes wrong, is this the way I will be remembered? "Remember"

"Remember"

"Remember"   "Remember"   "Remember"

I arrive at the water's edge of Hout Bay and I board the helicopter for the short flight. A minute in, I see Chapman's Peak Drive, which wraps itself around a mountain, rising high above the Atlantic Ocean. Looking below at the vast expanse of ocean, I can't help wondering about what awaits me beneath.

I finally reach my destination. Here is where I will embark on a journey of self-discovery. I am briefed again and all questions are answered. The boat floats gently and as I take a deep breath, the engines start. We journey into the murky oceans of my greatest fear. My mind relives my first viewing of *Jaws*.

INTELLECTUAL MAVERICK

FEAR IS JUST A MESSAGE

INTELLECTUAL
MAVERICK

My breathing patterns alter as I experience a restless silence. The stillness between my heartbeats is all that I can hear. We are in the middle of a vast expanse of water, totally at its mercy.

Inspecting the now, fragile looking cage.

There is an underlying tension that seems to intensify with each passing moment. I'm preparing for the dive, when totally by surprise, a Great White breaches with explosive energy. Its power is profound, as it effortlessly and gracefully slices through the air. For an instant I see the whole length of this remarkable creature.

I experience a moment of insecurity, then a sinking feeling as I climb into the cage; my sanctuary. I'm overwhelmed with emotion: the tension, the anticipation, a brief moment of composure and then tension again. The tables are turned; this time I am the one caged in their world. I feel as though I am trespassing and tampering with something sacred. Slowly I am lowered into the water, within seconds immersed in a timeless place. It's amazing how every cell of your being changes its state the minute you enter the water, knowing what awaits you.

Without warning I feel a powerful shift in the pressure of the water. Approaching me from my right is a Great White. It's approximately 15 metres away. At 10 metres it already looks four times its size; my confidence is diminished.

INTELLECTUAL MAVERICK

It begins to open its jaws as another shark joins it. I'm completely limp with fear as I question the strength of the now fragile-looking cage. All assurance fades away at 5 metres, 3 metres, 1 metre; I am now face to face with one of my greatest fears. Then I feel the pain, the pain of the mind fracture. All fear is crushed.

FEAR IS JUST A MESSAGE

I find myself in a place of silence, revealing the real me, a silence so deep, a silence so expansive and a silence that is so unveiling. There is a mysterious beauty in this moment of coming face to face with a Great White.

INTELLECTUAL
MAVERICK

The closer we are to death,

the more we feel alive

and alive

and alive .

It is within that impulse that creation takes place. It's a moment of freedom, an eternal revelation that crystallises you into eternity itself.

It's a moment of transparency and timeless wonder.

As the Great White circles the cage, I sense a different side to it. I devour the sights, sounds and sensations of the moment. It moves with an imposing power, yet also encompasses a placid, serene nature.

It truly is one of the most majestic beauties I've ever seen.

Factored into life:

Our crippling fears seem to exhibit those same quali- ties; they also seem to have an imposing power, yet they also encompass a placid, serene presence.

INTELLECTUAL MAVERICK

We can only **appreciate** our fears from a place of silence, from a depth **and timeless wisdom.**

FEAR IS JUST A MESSAGE

FEAR IS OUR

CONFLICT

WITH *TIME.*

Life is elusive,
time is magic
and
you
are the magician.

INTELLECTUAL
MAVERICK

You hold the timeless wisdom as you travel through the continuum of time to explore the deepest recesses of your psyche. To know yourself is to know that fear is not personal. All fear of failure or outcome, whether it's subtle or dominating, is not a part of you. You don't own it, nor does it own you.

FEAR IS
JUST A
MESSAGE

If we travelled to a place of silence; if we viewed with a depth and timeless wisdom, we'd arrive at the realisation that an undesired result is directly relative to the lack of intelligence in its process. Fear is the result of our neglect to gain insight into the process and actions of mitigating the risk.

INTELLECTUAL MAVERICK

If you employ a strategy that is not conducive to the results you seek, then you will not achieve the desired result. You have to understand that it's not you that has failed; it's just that you employed the wrong strategy. Fear is just an impulse; a quickening that tells you that your current strategy is probably not going to work. In these times, you will have to change your strategy so that you will be more confident in attaining the desired result.

Our fears engage us emotionally and create a greater degree of discord in terms of influencing our reactions, stifling our creativity and diluting our momentum. This leaves our minds in a very fragile state. The key to overcome this is to place your emphasis on gaining the insight and intelligence that you require to mobilise the circumstance into a successful outcome.

The purpose of this chapter is to offer you a basic frame of reference to serve as a support mechanism to strengthen your mind. The art of disengaging yourself emotionally and re-engaging yourself intellectually is the process of schooling your wits.

We need to gain an insight into ill-defined opportunities for the purpose of reinventing ourselves and leveraging our resourcefulness. **Strategy is a sequence of ideas that are meant to be mobilised in relation to the intention.**

Achieving success is never an idea in isolation. It is the composition and sequence of ideas that have to be mobilised to create the success. Our wits need to become schooled in order to enhance a clearer definition of what's required of us to mobilise our success.

We've all seen it time and again, where individuals rise out of the most devastating circumstances and transform their lives into greatness. If you are in a place where you feel that life's closing in on you, and you have a pressing urgency to transform your misfortune into another chance, then you have to make every effort to become more acquainted in the process of schooling your wits.

The results you seek have to be relative to the intelligent mobilisation of your intentions.

INTELLECTUAL MAVERICK

FEAR IS JUST A MESSAGE

Taking consistent action every day has to be done within the framework of the following definition. The *Jetstream* definition of "wits":

Investigative Skills,
Keen Perception,
Capacity to Quantify,
Ingenious Contrivance,
Risk Aversion
and Composure.

The more we integrate these insights and attributes into our consistent actions towards our success, the more we will find that luck will favour us, transforming our circumstances into another home run.

Investigative Skills

The starting point would be to investigate both successes and failures surrounding your specific circumstances. Studying successes will map your path forward, while studying failures will mark the landmines that you will need to navigate through. Don't investigate randomly. Your investigative processes should always be very specific to gain strategic insight. You will need to architect your findings into processes to mobilise the intelligence. Your constant investigation should help you to redefine your efforts more optimally, continuously dealing with the future as an instinctive exercise in foresight. Schooling your investigative skills will take you beyond the narrow mental activity of your fear, and it will develop your acumen and aptitude toward the successful mobilisation of your intentions.

Keen Perception

Your confidence can be disguised as a superficial confidence, which generally accelerates your tendency to make premature decisions. To take successful action requires you to place huge emphasis on what you don't know so that you can become more process-orientated and sophisticated in your approach

INTELLECTUAL MAVERICK

FEAR IS JUST A MESSAGE

to execute your plan with an informed definitive strength. To develop a keen perception is to place huge emphasis on your process of arriving at a conclusion, as opposed to the conclusion itself. Always evaluate the merits of your conclusion.

INTELLECTUAL MAVERICK

Capacity to Quantify

You need to place your focus on what needs to be done. It's all about the definition of actions and the mobilisation thereof. Your success is going to be determined by your consistent intelligent action that's within your management capabilities. We need to define our mission critical focus to bring structure, order and common sense to our efforts. Most importantly we need to be results orientated, which is our capacity to constantly quantify the progress we're making, so that we can influence the results we seek with our management skills.

Ingenious Contrivance

This is the process of stimulating and engaging your thoughts to optimise your creative and analytical genius.

Success *requires, a* **human touch,** intuitive powers *and* **provocative thinking processes**

INTELLECTUAL MAVERICK

to bring greater value to your actions. Ingenious contrivance creates the value within ill-defined opportunities, and negates the liability component.

FEAR IS JUST A MESSAGE

Risk Averse

We should never make an artificial interpretation of risk due to a lack of acquiring sufficient intelligence.

INTELLECTUAL MAVERICK

Being overwhelmed or unprepared for misfortune is largely due to a single-minded mental process. We should make every effort to evaluate our risk as comprehensively as possible, so that we are in a position to mitigate it optimally. The spectrum of risk ranges from ambiguous risk, volatile risk, conscious risk, and unconscious risk, to name but a few. The purpose of bringing this to your attention is so that you do not underestimate the proposed risk. In order for you to go forward successfully, you should always mitigate your risk of experiencing irreversible losses. Risk is contextual, which means that it's manageable. We need to always hold ourselves accountable to the way we **view, quantify and manage risk.**

Composure

When we are consumed with fear, our emotions scream so loudly that we can't contextualise our thought. This hinders our intellectual strategies as they become completely diluted with emotional chaos. The purpose of our strategy is to engineer outcome through the vibrancy of our intellectual processes. However, to assume that you are independent of the strategy would be intellectual suicide. How you behave within the strategy is probably more important than how your strategy behaves.

So relax,
because anxiety
does not
solve problems.

INTELLECTUAL MAVERICK

You need to develop the art of relaxing. I can't stress the importance enough, because you need to employ your still, calm and sharpened composure.

Most importantly, get a fair amount of sleep and get past self-defeating mentalities because as a criterion, the quality of concentration and effort that you invest into your strategy will determine your success.

INTELLECTUAL MAVERICK

Intelligence
is knowing
what's required
of us

so that we can frame the strength of its execution. You will find that the more you choose to face your fears, the greater will be your capacity to observe them. It's only when we view our fear with a depth and silence that we gain the insight towards our call to action. It's amazing how the human spirit is capable of overcoming even the most catastrophic circumstances. Irrespective of the circumstances that you find yourself in, it is highly improbable that the problem is unique to you.

There were and always will be people facing similar circumstances and conquering them. What's required is a sound framework of thinking, and this chapter was designed to offer you just that as a starting point.

We need to make every attempt to progressively exhibit a greater degree of wit in our everyday lives. Don't be alarmed and overwhelmed by your fears, just take a strategic stance and reinvent yourself exponentially. Listen to the message within fear, and articulate your quest to **IRREVOCABLY CHANGE YOUR WORLD.**

INTELLECTUAL MAVERICK

FEAR IS JUST A MESSAGE

The Taj Mahal

The Taj Mahal
The signature of love is everywhere

Now **we go in search of a**
truth.

A truth that oscillates within the depths of mystical
India, a peerless, ancient land, unrivalled in its beauty. To create more mystery and adventure, this truth
can only be revealed through the lens of your heart's
richest instincts. Together, you and I will embark on a
journey back in time, to the 17th century, to discover
a truth of the now.

We are on the streets of Mumbai, India. We flag down
a tuc-tuc and hesitantly take our seats. The driver takes
off, expertly weaving us between cars,
ox-carts, bicycles, buses and taxis. With
no road markings, it's obvious that there
is a secret order amongst all the pan-
demonium. We jerk to a halt as a group of beautiful
women brighten the street with an exotic fusion of
colour. Wrapped in scarlet, emerald green, turquoise
and gold saris, they walk through, barefooted and
smile pleasantly.

INTELLECTUAL MAVERICK

02:41:30 22

TO YOUR PODIUM FINISH

INTELLECTUAL MAVERICK

As we continue, we witness a city that's ruthless yet graceful, proud yet humble, longing yet utterly content. We drive past plush hotels elevated between slums. What you choose to see is entirely up to you.

We arrive at one of the local markets and are mesmerised by the surroundings. The hard gravel street is lined on either side with stalls. As we walk through, looking up, fresh-scented marigold garlands are draped in rows above us as far as we can see. We are eagerly approached by the merchants. They linger excitedly in the hope of a sale. The rich aromas of spices, curries and deep-fried pastries drifts through the air. Sweet local confectionaries in a delectable assortment of colours are being prepared before us.

Then, the sound of hypnotic music beckons us. We find ourselves before a snake charmer sitting on a tattered rug. He commands a cobra from its wicker basket, and it hypnotically sways to the sound of his flute.

A fine drizzle gently begins to fall, a kiss of refreshment relieving the humidity. We walk the streets, making inquiries about this great truth we seek, for you see, in order for this truth to be revealed you have to see it through a discerning mind. To view through the lens of our heart's richest instincts, we need someone who will awaken that degree of wakefulness within us to reveal the treasure within the truth.

INTELLECTUAL MAVERICK

We tempt the hand of fate.

We make inquiries in search of a legendary seer, whom many believe to be a myth. Our investigations lead us to an ancient temple; completely unaware that within the eternal possibilities that exist in that moment is the possibility of the seer discovering us. As fate goes on to reveal, through a tapestry of circumstances, he suddenly appears before us with more mystery than the now.

SIGNATURE OF LOVE

INTELLECTUAL MAVERICK

"I believe you were looking for me," *he says.*

We feel the hair on the back of our necks stand on end. "Well then, let me introduce myself. My name is Bangaar," which translated, means gold.

Before us stands an old man; his eyes sparkle as they reveal many lifetimes of wisdom, of tales and experiences.

He has long white hair that flows like an untamed river. He is dressed in a long robe that hides his feet, and moves as though he is floating. His appearance is an instant revelation that he is the person that we were searching for. What is so captivating about Bangaar is that he has a richness in his presence that extends beyond the translation of his name.

He has a commanding presence, yet his movements are gentle and passive as he clutches his bamboo cane. He gestures for us to take our seats; we lean in attentively as he far exceeds our expectation of mystery and intrigue.

He speaks in what can only be described as a collective medium that goes straight to and beyond the heart.

As I turn to my right, I see the sparkle in your eyes, confirming that you are just as blown away as I am. Then I hear your inquiring voice asking him to tell us the story of the Taj Mahal. In a low, hushed voice he begins.

INTELLECTUAL MAVERICK

SIGNATURE OF LOVE

One day as Shah Jahan was walking through the town, a window in time opened. He gazed into the eyes of a soul, a certain woman named Mumtaz, and their destinies became one in a place of timelessness. Their life together was an expression of the greatest passion, of wanting to share the experience of time.

*It was a place where the soul, **experienced** time through a soul.*

The potential that was awakened within these two souls transcended their love into a timeless fusion in what would unfold to be one of the greatest love stories, influencing countless lives to come. Elevated by love, Jahan and Mumtaz had an eternal view, which channelled their creativity into an appreciation of fine art.

After 19 years of marriage, tragedy struck. It was the year 1631, and Mumtaz welcomed their 14th child into the world. Their joy ended abruptly when they discovered that Mumtaz had suffered complications. Jahan grasped her hand in a knowing silence. Mumtaz whispered in his ear with a final breath for Jahan to reside in his passion by building a mausoleum as a testament of their great love for each other. Driven by the loss of his beloved, Jahan worked with a passion that consumed his waking hours. His new purpose was to capture the essence of his love in this legendary architecture. Jahan was able to create a significant monument to reveal to the world the love that he and his wife shared, an eternal love that even defies death; India's pride, the Taj Mahal.

INTELLECTUAL MAVERICK

SIGNATURE OF LOVE

As for Bangaar, he vanished into the reality of the now. All I can say for sure is that the experience was real, whether Bangaar was an answer; that can only be found in a self-reflective question.

WHAT IS LOVE?

Love is an awakening of everything from superficial ego to the *infinite*.

There is nothing tangible about love. There is nothing to understand in trying to define it. Most of society seems to struggle with the concept of a romantic love. Most romantic love is a translation of psyches. It's your partner's ability to bring out the better in you, resulting in you having a higher perception of yourself. You associate that higher perception of yourself with your partner, and you assume that you're in love with that person. However, in that moment of time, you are actually in love with yourself. As described, all relationships are actually three relationships; it's your partner's relationship with his-or herself, your relationship with yourself, and the relationship that you have with each other.

However, truth in life is determined by the relationship you have with yourself, because self-love is an expression of time. Self-love is one of life's prime rites of passage.

If love is an expression of time, then that means that you are an expression of time. You are the time in your life. What is the quality of this time?

.Life
is
so
precious.

It seems that we neglect to account for the importance of love in our everyday lives.

We as a society are caught up in a fast-paced world. We tend to be so preoccupied with our everyday lives that we become victims of our short-sighted and narrow-mindedness toward the value of expressing a greater measure of love. Inherently, we are a world within a world.

We need to exhibit an inner poise in spite of being comprehensively engaged in a fast-paced world. Our life is meant to offer us **contentment, peace, harmony, efficiency, ease and** happiness, but when we try and factor ourselves into these qualities, we find a poor fit due to our lack of expressions of love.

The love we seek refers to a variety of feelings, attitudes and states, and these are generally acquired by developing an unselfish concern for everything that represents life, as we know it.

INTELLECTUAL MAVERICK

SIGNATURE OF LOVE

INTELLECTUAL MAVERICK

The typical characteristics of someone that fails to awaken love oscillates more frequently into frustration, a victim mentality, they disempower their environments, are of heavier spirit and denser demeanour. Due to the fact that they are more inclined to carry a heavier spirit, they find that life is less rewarding and significantly more difficult.

In order for us to awaken our creativity, express our love, gratitude, contentment and happiness, we have to ground ourselves in a more comprehensive definition of love. We need to journey into the beauty that oscillates within the richness of life and this beauty is revealed by awakening the love that oscillates within the depth of us.

To awaken our richest instincts, to feel love, shape it, express it and to experience it in our everyday lives, we need to expand our awareness. We need to travel through a collective medium, straight through and beyond our hearts, a timeless fusion to discover the spatial dimensions and far reaches of the ocean of love within us.

The highest wisdom
is the realisation that the
signature
of
love
is everywhere.

INTELLECTUAL MAVERICK

The suggestion of this chapter is to experience the signature of love. Your true success is in the kaleidoscope of magic within your love. It's quite far reaching to assume that we can achieve this expansiveness, but what if we travelled in the vehicle of words?

What if we travelled at the speed of thought?

Let's give it a shot.

Love is:

A passion, a feeling, an impulse and a whisper. It's an awakening, a clarity, a smile, laughter, joy, a glimmer of light. It is peace, harmony, a wish, hope and a blessing amidst the chaos. **Love** is courage, fear, curiosity, a discovery, a celebration and a victory. It's also defeat, it's surrendering oneself. LOVE is reality. It is people, events, circumstances, moments, memories and trust. It's a burning desire and charm. Love is enchanting and captivating. It's an appreciation, an understanding and commitment. It's a vision, speculation, a strategy, a time frame, vigour and synchronicity.

It's life cycles. LOVE is found in good fortune and tragedy. It's friendship and discipline, it's magic, spirit, enthusiasm and magnetic. It's a snowflake, a flame, a zest, a grandeur and being alive. It's an aspiration, a motive and an experience. It's an enquiry of time, awareness and results. It's a beat, a rhythm, a pulse and vibrations.

INTELLECTUAL MAVERICK

It's endearing and conflicting.

SIGNATURE OF LOVE

Love is waves and stillness, extravagance and simplicity, a practice and inspiration. Love is spontaneity, a test and a quest. It's acquisition, currency, wealth, resources, business and challenges. It's happiness, contentment, indulgence and triumph; it's a jewel, a crown, a treasure, eternal. It's also tears and it's pain.

INTELLECTUAL MAVERICK

IT'S ONLY
WHEN WE ARE ABLE TO
EXCEED OUR
RIGID INTERPRETATIONS,
AND WE START
DEFINING LOVE
IN ITS
TOTALITY,
THAT WE REALISE'
THAT LOVE
IS
EVERYWHERE.

Love surrounds you, it envelops you and it embraces you. Love is everywhere you go. You cannot escape it. If you go to the ends of the earth, it's there. You'll find it at the bottom of the deepest oceans, in the darkest abyss of your greatest fears, the highest mountain peak. It's in the kiss of the faintest breeze, in the scent of a solitary rose, in the song of a bird. Love is in a sunset, in a moonrise. It's the sound of thunder, a bolt of lightning, in the dance of a wave, in the stillness of a moment. It's in the cry and laughter of a child, in the silent gaze of a parent, a mother's healing kiss, a father's secure embrace. It's in the outstretched hands of a beggar, in the lost eyes of an orphan, in the aged person's aching call for attention. It's in a sportsman's victory, in a nation's struggle, in an orchestra of music. Love is in the movement of the stars. Love is in a gesture. It is in a prayer. Love permeates and pulsates in every atom of existence.

INTELLECTUAL
MAVERICK

GOD IS LOVE.
The signature of love is everywhere.

And in this wakefulness, you will find yourself
in a sunrise, in a raindrop, in a stranger's smile,
in a thought, in a breath, in a silence. You will find
yourself in the total. You will find yourself
in the unknown elegance that
orchestrates everything in life.
Envision for a boundless second,
being in this elevated state,

THEN THE WORLD TRULY BECOMES

GRANDIOSE.

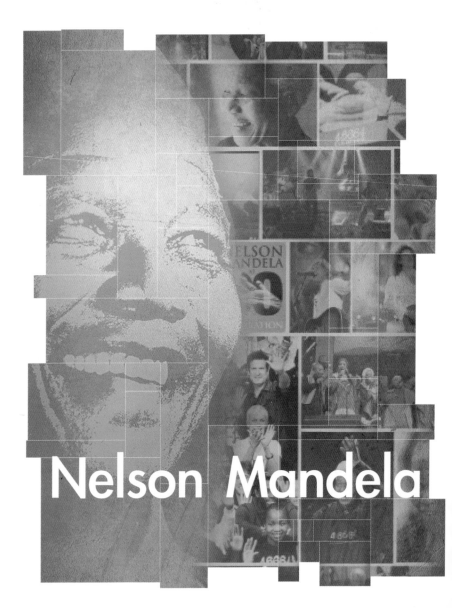

Nelson Mandela

Nelson Mandela

We are prisoners of our habits

46664 were the numbers given to the new inmate at the Robben Island prison. For the rest of his imprisonment he would be reduced to the nameless, being called number 46664. At the time, prisoners were given their number based on the date of their arrival followed by the last two digits of the year. Nelson Mandela was the 466th person to arrive at Robben Island prison in the year 1964.

INTELLECTUAL MAVERICK

Today, I find myself at Nelson Mandela's "46664" 90th birthday concert in London's Hyde Park. Helicopter searchlights flood the evening sky, as they hover above us. Camera crews are on the sidelines, recording the event that will be televised worldwide. Photographers are capturing each moment from every possible angle. Fans are filling the park in a steady flow. The hype and excitement escalating around me.

BECOME EXTRAORDINARY

01:53:02

TO YOUR PODIUM FINISH

Tonight Josh Groban, Queen and Leona Lewis are some of the artists scheduled to perform. It's a very humbling experience to attend one of Mandela's "46664" concerts.

The moment Nelson Mandela stepped on to that Hyde Park stage, the crowd gave an enthusiastic cheer. He gazed at the crowd with a kind, fatherly look, and then he made a triumphant gesture,

INTELLECTUAL MAVERICK

HIS FIST RAISED.

The impact that he had on the crowd was truly overwhelming.

This is a man who sacrificed so much of his life. He gestured for us to settle down. As he began to speak, a silence fell on the crowd. We listened attentively, wanting to take in every word. His expression was serene. He spoke briefly, calmly, and humbly. As I listened to him, I found it difficult to comprehend his life experiences.

On the 10th of May 1994, Nelson Mandela was inaugurated as South Africa's first democratically elected president. It was a very proud moment as he made his acceptance speech. Mandela personifies the word victory; he was an anti-apartheid activist who suffered the consequences by being banned, arrested and imprisoned. His most severe punishment came when he was sentenced to 27 years of imprisonment. Mandela was transferred to Robben Island prison where he spent 18 of the 27-year sentence. At the age of 71,

Mandela
was finally a free man.

INTELLECTUAL MAVERICK

He has received more than 100 awards in 4 decades, including the Nobel Peace Prize. As the world's most famous political prisoner, he exhibits a moral integrity that shines far beyond South Africa. This is a man that has taken great risks and has sacrificed his personal life and youth to achieve democracy and equality.

I couldn't help but wonder what state of mind Mandela was in, witnessing an arena filled with supporters. I asked myself - how does one go from being a prisoner for decades,

TO BECOMING ONE OF THE WORLD'S MOST HEROIC FIGURES?

WE ARE PRISONERS OF OUR HABITS.

INTELLECTUAL MAVERICK

Upon closer examination of society's lifestyle and behaviour, it becomes increasingly apparent that we all live within very limited paradigms. It seems that we are prisoners of our habits, but that's not the tragedy. The real tragedy is that we are completely oblivious to this fact, resulting in us being held captive and chained to our habits. It seems that we are incapable of noticing the routines of our behaviour, and the repetitive nature of our thinking, because the repetition is subconscious. The routine nature of our lifestyles undermines our

self-analytical mental muscles

and we refuse to respond to the stimuli that our days present us. A clinical interpretation will reveal that, given a period of time, our routine lifestyle does not stimulate us enough to respond to with any significant influence. It seems that our responses become more inclined toward automatic reactions as opposed to influential reactions.

LIFE
IS OPULENTLY
EXTRAVAGANT.

INTELLECTUAL
MAVERICK

Each day unlocks doors to such richness and depth, magic and elegance. Life streams such profound simplicities and orchestrated beauty. Life is simply extraordinary, but we ourselves need to become extraordinary in order to access this magic. We lose our appetite for life and discount our view of it when we get diluted in the process of settling for basic daily entertainment and our effort to maintain a reasonable lifestyle.

INTELLECTUAL MAVERICK

In our quest for short-term comforts, we unconsciously simplify our lives to such basic demands that we fail to act on opportunities that offer us the stimulation and self-engagement that Steve Jobs was referring to when he said, "Stay hungry, stay foolish." Stay foolish in this context basically means that if you feel that you know everything, you will never be open to learn. Jobs advises us to stay foolish so that we will acquire the attitude that allows us the freedom to learn. The essence of this chapter is referring to your capacity to self-negotiate. When we lack self-negotiation, then we simplify and discount the extravagance of life.

We need to develop an appetite for life. Learning how to self-negotiate will make us alive to a symphony of opportunity that is conducive to a lifestyle of success. Our capacity to self-negotiate is what will take us beyond our limited mental activity and allow us to experience the freedom of life.

When we are careless or neglectful about the way we self-negotiate our efforts to succeed, then we fall victim to our lack of awareness. Some common shortfalls are:

Conservativeness

Is an attitude that favours retaining a traditional approach to life. You are a traditionalist in terms of seeking to preserve things the way they are, in order to maintain stability and continuity.

Indulgence

The acts of replacing high priority actions with tasks of lower priority for the sake of immediate enjoyment, thus neglecting important tasks.

Procrastination

You believe that life will offer you a second chance. It's called tomorrow. Unfortunately for you, the future is created in the now.

INTELLECTUAL MAVERICK

Weak Attitude

In this context, attitude towards life has been ill-defined, and as a result, one could very likely develop an unfavourable attitude towards life.

Gradualism

You'll find that factored into life,

a gradual approach is most inclined to resist change.

Transformation and the creation of successes, generally requires oceans of energy and commitment. Be sure to adjust to the required pace.

Dilution

Consciously or unconsciously wasting your own time and dissipating your energy. This is where you spend an excessive amount of time on any given aspect that is not conducive to your progress. It could be anything that you indulge in that dilutes your attention, but I'm not talking about you; I'm talking about the other seven billion people that you feel need to get off their lazy bums and make you the success you were destined to be. Just kidding. On a more serious note, become more aware of the way you allocate your time. Your time means everything, it's imperative that it should be part of your management tools.

Time should always be *employed in your favour.*

INTELLECTUAL MAVERICK

BECOME EXTRAORDINARY

INTELLECTUAL
MAVERICK

I'm sure you will agree that it's becoming more obvious that self-negotiation is of utmost importance. There is no specific key to self-negotiation, but one of the simplest ways to school yourself in the process is to find various role models. This basic initiative merely offers you points of reference or benchmarks to measure yourself against.

The level of success you achieve in life will be largely determined by your capacity to weave and create the fabric of your self-negotiation skills.

Having appropriate role models will help you crystallise the criteria that should underpin your actions as you move towards your proposed success.

FRAME YOUR FUTURE SUCCESSES

Our lives are going to play out within a sequence of events, opportunities, setbacks, joys, pains and celebrations. Depending what our quests are, we can decide what dose of the following components we require. Use role models to factor the following into your life:

Progressivism

Defining our lifestyle to advocate our reform. Self-development and advanced changes should be your game plan. The principles we live by should always offer us a degree of flexibility to expand our lives and mobilise our successes as daily choices and practices.

Taking Responsibility

This is our capacity to avoid complacency. We have an obligation to become the director of our lives. Taking responsibility is being able to listen very intently, and then gaining the insights to mobilise our progress. The greatest hurdle here is that we – both individuals and

INTELLECTUAL MAVERICK

BECOME EXTRAORDINARY

INTELLECTUAL MAVERICK

society as a whole – often find it difficult to accept and apply the findings of self-criticism because we tend to believe in our own perfection. This attitude will cause us to discount many of the spectrum of messages that life offers us daily. Being able to see every single person as our teacher is what will allow us to be open to our development.

Questing to become extraordinary

"It's madness, absolute craziness, inconceivable, virtually impossible, and insurmountable." That's the criticism and the odds that every extraordinary person faces on their path to greatness. In hindsight, it's easy to look at these individuals and say that they are extraordinary, but they may once have been unknown and penniless; their only possession being their vault of ideas. Can you imagine how reckless they would have seemed to us, thinking that they could achieve greatness? How can an individual be so bold as to think he can achieve so much more than his fellow humans? You are one of those people. The sooner you accept it, the sooner you begin to re-invent yourself.

Being extraordinary is about cultivating the divinely conferred power of your intention. It's you developing a compelling attraction towards seemingly impossible goals, hence developing a greater charm and charisma toward the actions of its attainment.

INTELLECTUAL MAVERICK

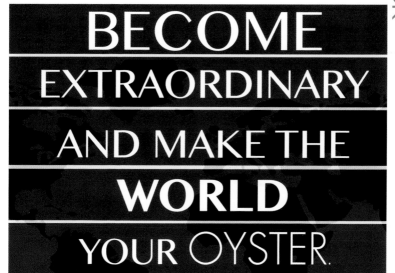

BECOME
EXTRAORDINARY
AND MAKE THE
WORLD
YOUR OYSTER.

Commitment

INTELLECTUAL MAVERICK

Commitment, as self-explanatory as it may sound, is insanity without basic management tools. Being able to define our commitment relative to the proposed value of return should always be the primary focus of our commitment. Your commitment should be defined by its merits. The ability to

quantify your level
of commitment required,

relative to your current and projected position, is what maps the degree of your sanity, always bearing in mind that your plans to achieve don't have to make sense to the world - but they do have to make sense to you. Our acumen and aptitude should be employed unceasingly to ensure that our commitment is always a part of a conscious deliberate process.

Acumen and Aptitude

SWING
FOR
THE
FENCES.

INTELLECTUAL MAVERICK

You are in the game of life every day. Your process and timing of achievement is going to be directly relative to the degree of acumen and aptitude that you apply. The quickness and accuracy in your mental processes is what will determine your level of insight, enabling you to make an astute judgment of the opportunities presented, and to re-create them in a form that will yield strategic gains. The following statement is so important that I have to repeat it. Intelligence is knowing what's required of you so that you can factor yourself into life.

It just makes more sense to find ways to have role models wherever possible. That will simply make us more mindful of where we are as opposed to where we need to be, so that we can factor ourselves into the process of achievement.

Be sure to always live a "life in progress". Engineer your life so that it becomes more meaningful to you with each passing year. Plan your celebrations and aim toward specific victories. Employ time in your favour. Take a stance, choose a direction, and

INTELLECTUAL
MAVERICK

BECOME THE SUCCESS YOU WERE DESTINED TO BE.

Captain of
Your Life

Captain of Your Life
The future will arrive

INTELLECTUAL MAVERICK

It was an impulsive break away from college to the clear waters and white sandy beaches of the island of Mauritius, a group of friends, with just our duffel bags, and zero agenda.

After endless nights of clubbing and lazy days on the beach, we spent our final night at a beach party, where liberal amounts of alcohol were consumed. Our flight was scheduled to leave at 7 a.m.; sleepless, we grabbed our luggage and negotiated with the taxi driver to get us to the airport on time.

AWAKEN YOUR DYNAMISM

Exhausted from the night before, we hauled ourselves through to the check-in counter. The weather conditions were dreadful, with a combination of heavy winds and hammering rain.

01:05:29:07
TO YOUR PODIUM FINISH

INTELLECTUAL
MAVERICK

We were impatient and desperate to get home. As we made our way out to the plane there was a piercing-cold wind. We got on board and began to move down the aisle, anxious to get to our seats. All the passengers settled in and shortly after we began preparing for take-off.

There was an upsurge of engine noise as we began to gain momentum on the runway, and the fierce wind, ripped and tugged at the plane. It was then that I began to have doubts about whether we would have a safe flight.

The tension was steadily mounting. As we looked anxiously out of the cabin windows, we could see angry bolts of lightning strike through the walls of thick mist. We were now in severe turbulence at approximately ten thousand feet, and my confidence was completely shaken. I watched the colour drain from the cabin crew's faces, as they exchanged urgent whispers. My overriding emotion was now fear.

At fifteen thousand feet, the passengers were exchanging horrified gasps as we were being jolted back and forth. At twenty thousand feet there was a note of panic in everyone's voices. The beverage trollies went hurtling down the aisle. At twenty five thousand feet, desperation began to set in. The plane was being thrown from side to side, and we were left helpless; our fate undecided.

Imagine weather conditions that were literally threatening to break the wings off the plane! I think at that point, each one of us on board was silently praying that we would make it back home safely.

Our prayers were answered. Eventually, at thirty thousand feet, the plane reached calmer air. All around, I could hear sighs of relief. Then, a perfectly calm, confident voice came over the intercom and said: "Ladies and gentlemen, this is your captain speaking."

INTELLECTUAL
MAVERICK

"We apologise for the bumpy take-off, which was the result of heavy turbulence. We will be out of the turbulence in the next few minutes and we will be met with clear blue skies. Our estimated flight time is six hours. Enjoy the rest of your flight."

His calmness and confidence neutralised our concerns. His demeanour reassured everyone that we would have a safe flight after all. It was then that I remembered a joke from my childhood and thought to myself, what would have happened if the captain had emerged from the cockpit, distraught and wearing a parachute, saying, "Don't panic, I'm going for help!"

It made me realise that we are the captains of our lives, and the manner in which we strategise and act on each day is what determines a journey of success. The human instinct is always trying to establish a degree of certainty. If you are looking for certainty, then you can be assured that the future will arrive. The question is, where will you arrive in the next five years?

YOU ARE THE CAPTAIN OF YOUR LIFE.

When you are navigating through life, you have to do it from a PLACE OF EXCELLENCE. The most important question is: What are you using to navigate? We navigate by using our dynamism. The way we factor ourselves into life is the process of navigating through various comprehensive definitions with the intention to mobilise our interests. There is a dynamic that takes us from our current circumstances to our greatest dreams and that dynamic hinges on the structural framework of our DECISIONS.

What is a decision?

A DECISION IS AN IMPULSE TOWARDS CHANGE.

Can change be measured? The answer is a resounding YES! If change can be measured, that means your decisions can be measured, because the quality of your decision influences the extent of your change. If one acquires the art of navigating using one's dynamism, then one can accelerate the achievement process well beyond expectation.

The big question then becomes: How do we demystify the seemingly complex nature of our decision-making processes?

We all seem to employ our decisions, and often walk away unclear as to what frames their merits. The diversity of decisions does not necessarily apply equally to the lifecycles of our success. We need to decipher a basic definition of the range in decisions and assess the value that they offer. We tend to stand by and justify our decisions, often not clearly understanding their criteria.

INTELLECTUAL MAVERICK

AWAKEN YOUR DYNAMISM

YOUR DECISIONS WILL RE-ROUTE YOUR FUTURE.

INTELLECTUAL MAVERICK

A decision is not a choice of either or; it's not as simple as just a yes or no. It's the definition of dynamics of intentions, and then mobilising the interest. A decision is a fulcrum, allowing you to associate one of two choices, and then threading through the eye of the intention to go forward exponentially. It's a place of truth where you define where you are challenged to go. It's an insight into the action and motion of re-creating. It's the realisation of being at the cusp of a new frontier.

A decision is a place of strength,
established through

THE ART OF AWAKENING YOUR

DYNAMISM.

INTELLECTUAL MAVERICK

Awakening your dynamism is a process of recognition; the recognition that a decision marks a start and not an end. Think about it for a moment. Your decisions are relative to what?

They're
relative
to
opportunity.

What is an opportunity?

INTELLECTUAL MAVERICK

It is the recognition of information.

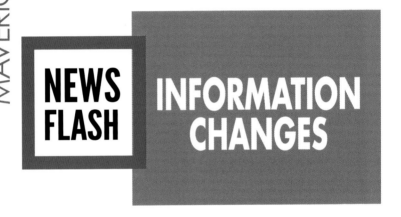

NEWS FLASH **INFORMATION CHANGES**

If your decision was based on information and subsequently, the information changed, then shouldn't the range of your decisions change? So you see, a decision is not a fixed, rigid concept. It's an oscillating truth that can only be discovered through the eye of time. Your decisions have to be relative to your evolving criteria for opportunity.

If you take a closer look at some of the types of decisions listed below, you will be able to analyse with greater awareness and accuracy which decisions most closely resemble the context of your success.

Emotional Decisions

In making emotional decisions, we are influenced by emotional interpretations of circumstances. Sophisticated thinkers are generally strongly opposed to making emotional decisions, but there is some merit in allowing a degree of emotion into the exceptional cases. In that event you have to create the most appropriate blend to define your decisions and, as a minimum requirement, you will need to write the circumstance down, get it out of your head, onto paper in a step-by-step format, so that you are able to analyse it more comprehensively.

You need to be able to answer these questions as a minimum requirement pertaining your decision:

INTELLECTUAL MAVERICK

What's the possible loss?

What's the possible gain?

What's the nature of the risk?

How does it affect your
current position?

Can you recover from
the adverse exposure?

Speculative Decisions

There are times when we are expected to reach a conclusion without the luxury of adequate information. It is at these times that our insight is discounted and we find ourselves vulnerable to the inadequate information being volunteered in spite of our processes. The challenge then becomes to make the decision without the sophistication of a proven formula.

It's at this point that we turn to mathematics as we try to calculate the probability and scope of possible outcomes. The greatest caution here is our bias, in that we see what we want to see, which could potentially influence the result of our calculation, which in turn could offer little or no merit in determining the actual probability amplitude of projected events.

If you find that you envisaged any reward related outcome correctly, then your greatest exponential future risk becomes yourself.

You see, most people are unaware that when we speculate correctly, the brain secretes a natural chemical called dopamine, which creates a natural high and feeling of euphoria.

This feeling is addictive, and as a result, you could potentially become addicted to your speculations. This type of decision, by nature, lacks insight, which inevitably will blindly lead you to substantial losses. You have to realise that your speculation is simply gambling your way through life, so make every effort to minimise the use of speculative decisions.

INTELLECTUAL MAVERICK

Reactive Decisions

Reactive decisions are our human tendency to want to optimise timing and reward. We throw a web of reach on the oscillating opportunity and the associated opportunities in order to capitalise and capture greater value. Our efforts are geared to optimise the results we seek. However, the danger is that reactive decisions are generally quick and not contemplated, so if you make a reactive decision, be sure to revisit it until you are totally confident and convinced that it is the correct one. Don't be motivated to prove your decisions right, but rather, be motivated to arrive at them through the correct processes.

Proactive Decisions

Proactive decisions are ones that follow a rigorous investigative process to seek successful future outcomes. Their purpose is to define the actions that will lead to the desired results. Proactive decisions offer us the greatest chance of success in life because they map resources and engineer our thought processes to meet our goal dependencies and goal congruencies. Proactive decisions are ones where you become very process orientated.

You define the target, and take the intellectual shot.

INTELLECTUAL MAVERICK

AWAKEN YOUR DYNAMISM

INTELLECTUAL MAVERICK

Most people are unaware of the importance of defining the target. It's intellectual suicide to think that you can take a shot at a target you can't define. Proactive thinking involves a clear definition, a sequence of ideas and a stitching of those insights to create strategic opportunity. It is a very structured and thoughtful process to frame your success in its various lifecycles, and thereafter, to package those ideas to mobilise the actions to produce the results. In general,

WE MINE
OUR GREATEST
VALUE
THROUGH THE PROCESS
OF
PROACTIVE THINKING.

MAKE EVERY EFFORT TO RESIDE
IN THIS STATE OF MIND.

Programmed Decisions

Programmed decisions are generally taken within established policies, either personal or corporate. The purpose is to make their influence as routinely sequential as possible. A programmed decision is assumed to have a certain amount of intelligence, but if the decision was made from a place of ignorance, then panic would be in order.

So don't be blind to the suggestion of programmed decisions, especially if such a decision doesn't hold any water in intellectual and/or economic terms. Don't be a blind follower, think before following, or better still, be a leader. Make sure your programmed decisions are motivated correctly, and be sure to give yourself meaningful choices as you strive to achieve greater things.

INTELLECTUAL MAVERICK

AWAKEN YOUR DYNAMISM

Indecision

Indecision is taking a hindsight approach. It's often a symptom of lack of motivation. The basic way to evaluate this is to analyse your motivation. If you are indecisive due to lack of motivation, then you will be inclined to aspire to mediocre or below average results. The most successful personalities define where they need to go, and what's required of them, and they take the actions relative to the results they seek. That is the main quality that accounts for their success. If you investigated further, you'd find that indecisiveness comes from two areas.

The first is the unconvincing odds of gain; that is where you feel the probability of achieving the result is minimal. The second is a lack of insight due to having insufficient information. However, in a fast-paced world, your indecision really amounts to a decision - to leave the game while it is in progress.

If there are no merits in taking a particular opportunity, then you should be very decisive to create new opportunities. So your mission should be to translate indecision into decision.

Life is not as obvious as applying a specific principle and getting everything you desire. You will, however, find that the more comprehensively you make a decision, the more your chances of achieving a greater degree of success. We are a life in progress, and we should become more alive to our decisions, and especially to the circumstances pertaining them. It would be a dire error to assume that a decision marks an end; because the reality is that any decision you make actually marks a starting point.

A DECISION
IS YOUR CALL TO ACTION.

It's the mobilisation of your interest, it's forward thinking and a stitching together of insights, and most importantly, it's your management acumen.

INTELLECTUAL MAVERICK

A DECISION IN ISOLATION MEANS NOTHING.

INTELLECTUAL MAVERICK

Anyone can make a decision, whether through a sophisticated process or not, but, super achievers always authenticate their decisions and are well aware that the execution of the decision is where their genius resides. The sophisticated process of making a decision and then executing it has to be done within an intellectual framework. The framework I am referring to is your criteria. You must have criteria to make a decision, and in terms of the execution, you need to have criteria to measure the progress against. Without criteria, all decision and effort is just random and unjustified. The success you achieve in your initiatives will be directly proportional to how comprehensively you define the underpinning criteria of your decisions.

The opposite of resignedly accepting "fate" and "destiny" is being the captain of your life. It is being able to take your circumstances and use your criteria for making decisions to generate new maps while quantifying and managing the execution. In the same way that a pilot uses the instruments to measure the various dynamics of the flight, you should use your criteria for your decisions as your instruments. This will allow you to see whether the required dynamics of your execution are in equilibrium.

INTELLECTUAL MAVERICK

Being the captain of your life is being able to map your path and create your future. It's taking that leap towards a life in progress. So get on board and brace yourself to

FLY

ON SELF-ENGAGEMENT.

AWAKEN YOUR DYNAMISM

MAP YOUR PATH
AND CREATE YOUR

FUTURE.

LEGENDS CREATE HISTORY EVERYDAY

THE
JETSTREAM

INSPIRED BY HUMANITY

YOU ARE THE INSPIRATION

Monaco

Monaco
Life becomes a race

I'm on the deck of a Ferretti yacht docked at Monaco for the Grand Prix, with the taste of a Davidoff Dom Perignon cigar on my lips. I'm privileged to be a part of this amazing spectacle. To the East, rows of custom-designed yachts, like luxurious floating villas, nod on the Mediterranean. To the South lies the turquoise sea, rippling out to a glorious horizon, and to the North, Monaco, undoubtedly the diamond of the world. Hugged by the mountains and kissed by the sea. It's the most breathtaking exhibition of unsurpassed extravagance that could overwhelm even the most lethargic of souls. Monaco is a city that exudes the seductive allure of wealth, glamour and power. The richly preserved history, the culturally opulent architecture and the unreserved modern sophistication contribute to the infectious energy that's associated with success.

INTELLECTUAL MAVERICK

CHAMPION YOUR LIFE

00:27:13 03
TO YOUR PODIUM FINISH

INTELLECTUAL MAVERICK

As I lounge on the deck, I see the familiar faces of some of the jet-setters. The escalating buzz of the media heralding another Grand Prix.

Race day at Monaco.

Monaco is renowned for its Formula One Grand Prix that it has hosted annually since 1929. Considered one of the most prestigious automobile races of the world, the spectacle and glamour result in the race being the jewel of the Formula One crown.

Fans travel from all over the world to witness this sporting and social event where the city streets are transformed into a challenging racetrack. The racecourse has many sudden elevation changes, sharp corners and tight hairpin bends, making it one of the most demanding circuits in the world of Formula One racing. The design of the circuit pushes the drivers to their limits; testing their talent over the power of the car.

Imagine being surrounded by a sea of contagiously fanatical supporters along a scorching dry track. The cars are at their starting positions and you can literally feel the vibrations of the sounds of the engines beneath your feet. As the lights signal the start of the race, the sound becomes deafening as the cars accelerate towards the first corner. The crowd goes ballistic and all you can see is a red ocean of Ferrari supporters. It is as though the effort of their cheers adds to the force of the engines.

Formula One is a sport renowned for its high stakes. It's a sport of precision, mobilisation of intelligence, processes of performance, optimisation, endurance, commitment and efficiency, to mention a few. Formula One is about the human skill applied to the unyielding quest for championship. The podium is reserved for the best of the best; it's one of the most expensively extreme sports that's technologically driven, and winning, most times, is determined by split second decisions.

Formula One is about defining the limits of performance, the intelligence in strategy and the dominance of reliability, and then exceeding them.

This chapter is intended to offer you a competitive advantage in life. We culminate with the Monaco Grand Prix to help you identify with the concept of life at full throttle.

INTELLECTUAL MAVERICK

Life is what you make of it. It goes by in a flash. We find that as we reach our more mature lifecycles, we don't regret our setbacks, our heartbreaks or our failures as much as we regret the opportunities that we failed to act upon. We spend our whole lives gaining knowledge. It almost seems to be an unspoken quest, but there will be a day when you will realise that knowledge in isolation offers no value. With any luck - let's hope that day is today.

Legends create history everyday. They chase seemingly impossible goals, sound in the wisdom that it's not the goal that matters, but who they become in the process of achieving that goal.

Legends are those people who realise that one would have to evolve mentally, emotionally and spiritually in order to

MATERIALISE THE SEEMINGLY

INTELLECTUAL MAVERICK

IMPOSSIBLE.

CHAMPION YOUR LIFE

In our attempt to learn, to experience, to grow, to live to the full, we become increasingly aware that time is against us. If we are trying to progress in our lives, relative to time, then:

LIFE BECOMES A RACE.

INTELLECTUAL
MAVERICK

The result of your race is determined by your learning *curve.*

Most societies are unaware of their learning curves. The learning curve is the experiential application of knowledge. It is the acceleration of developing one's acumen through the application of that knowledge. The learning curve is actually the distilled wisdom extracted in our quest to accelerate our lives towards meaningful goals.

The opposite of a Formula One attitude is a neutral demeanour, idle mentality, complacent attitude, unmotivated aspirations, a casual approach and a lack of a sense of championship. Whether you realise it or not, or you chose to accept it or ignore it, it doesn't change the fact that you are still in a race. Most of society will stand afar and either marvel at, or envy the achievements of others in all arenas of success. However, we need to realise that we are all on the same track heading towards our own personal goals.

INTELLECTUAL MAVERICK

ALL ACCOMPLISHMENT IS THE RESULT OF A CHOICE.

CHAMPION YOUR LIFE

The unyielding commitment to the practice of self-engagement makes champions. The constant practice and mastering of the use of **KEY PERFORMANCE INDICATORS**, frames successes.

We need to define our Key Performance Indicators.

INTELLECTUAL MAVERICK

We all want to live a life of progress where we achieve the results we seek. We need to evaluate our goals and gain a clear definition of what actions are required of us in the short-term in order to secure long-term successes. In corporate business, the term used to describe the definition and the measurement of the rate of progress is called Key Performance Indicators.

Now when you consider the business of your life, it becomes a necessity to define your Key Performance Indicators comprehensively, to serve as an instrument to frame your actions and measure your performance against. What you have in life is a direct reflection of your capacity to define your KPIs. If you find yourself lacking in any area of life, it would be largely due to ill-defined KPIs. We need to make intelligent demands on ourselves and our KPIs are meant to serve that purpose. Always be mindful that all success is determined by holding yourself accountable to your Key Performance Indicators.

WE NEED TO **GAIN** INSIGHT TO TAKE DEFINITIVE **ACTIONS.**

Champions are not people that pride themselves on knowledge in isolation; these are people who pride themselves on self-engagement that results in intelligent actions.

To these outstanding individuals, it's more a process of mental gymnastics, of taking that knowledge, stress-testing it, analysing it and seeking results, creating new scenarios to test behavioural changes and re-casting their findings to create a competitive advantage.

They define the limits of optimisation, performance and endurance, and then exceed them; whether it's in the field of spiritual development or materialistic goals, the practice of successful attitudes in all arenas - all share similar traits. All of us need to give our lives championship qualities by extracting the intelligence from knowledge pertaining to our goals and then consistently mobilising a life of achievement.

The process that a Formula One driver employs to become a champion is to master the art of focusing on the apex, driving line, braking, his latent talent versus the horsepower of the car, over-steering, counter-steering, track conditions and competing drivers, to name but a few. Every day, these drivers go onto the track with one intention, and that is to improve their **learning curve.**

Due to the high stakes in Formula One racing, the drivers have to intently study every detail of the track. We need to have the same awareness because we are all at the starting position of our next life cycle with the track of life before us. Practicing a Formula One attitude will allow us to assess opportunity more keenly and thus improve our performance.

If you want to emulate the **Formula One Attitude,** then you have to assess the track before you. You have to look at your life holistically and evaluate your goals. Achieving success in all arenas of your life is not determined by fate or chance. You are required to influence the outcome with passion, elegance and intelligence that is conducive to your progress.

When you consider the decades before you, you'll re-alise that life requires more than a whisper of wisdom. Life will demand a lot of you and you will have to be sure to deliver. The future will not afford you the luxury of ill-defined milestones that undermine the intelligence of a convincing definitive effort.

Life can be both predictable and spontaneous. In-evitably, we are going to experience highs and lows, stresses and silences, but irrespective of the quality of the time, it seems that we are constantly being play-fully challenged to take a shot at what seems to be progressively moving targets.

Our goals are constantly being engi-neered by our efforts, and our problems will always be masked by symptoms. With this being said, life plays out as a karmic game to develop self-mastery.

INTELLECTUAL MAVERICK

CHAMPION YOUR LIFE

INTELLECTUAL MAVERICK

It seems that the game requires us to develop an astute capacity to reinvent ourselves so that we can factor ourselves more intelligently and as a result more optimally into our game plan.

Again, the instrument to serve your intelligence in your convincing definitive effort is called Key Performance Indicators.

The Jetstream of Success has been written to reveal the ill-defined goals and conversely, the chapters can be used to help you design your KPIs in a way that is conducive to a comprehensive life in progress.

The characteristics attributed to champions are:

DEFINITIVE INTENT   SELF-ACCOUNTABILITY

RISK AVERSION   STUDENT OF YOUR HISTORY

STRATEGIC PLANNING   **INDEPENDENT THINKING**

MEDITATIVE GRATITUDE   ANALYTICAL GENIUS

INTELLIGENT ACTIONS   **INVESTIGATIVE SKILLS**

WITH THE CAPACITY TO REINVENT THEMSELVES.

All of these qualities are enhanced when measured against your KPIs. To personify these qualities requires huge motivation and commitment, together with clear points of reference, but most importantly, the actions we take, represented by the

Key Performance Indicators, have to be **conducive** to the **results** we **seek.**

I can't emphasise the importance enough; the lack of results we seek are largely due to ill-defined KPIs. You need to make every initiative to read between the lines of the chapters to extract the full value of its merits. The result of this process will school your thinking, acumen and your intelligence, helping you to reach specific goals and add value to your life. It will also help you develop the emotional disciplines to avoid setbacks.

Championing your life forward is your capacity to place huge emphasis on your learning curve. Always be sure to remember that intelligence is knowing what's required of you. As a rule, you should never approach this process as an aggressive need to reinvent yourself, because above all, life is meant to be loved for its infinite beauty, and reinventing yourself in context requires character, patience and commitment.

The high-stakes nature of the intelligence
presented in this book will help you develop a
Formula One attitude,
and the practice thereof will allow you
to experience life at full throttle.

**The spirit in me honours the spirit in you.
Many thanks,**

Julian Pencilliah

**SUCCESS
IS A
PLACE
IN TIME...**DON'T BE LATE

Acknowledgements

INTELLECTUAL MAVERICK

A special thank you to every single person in *The Jetstream* team across all of our offices globally who have influenced the creation of *The Jetstream* on all the various online and off-line platforms.
www.thejetstream.com/team

Many thanks to the companies that have partnered with us in the development of our online products:

Virtustream USA, Dotsquares USA, Wildfire Interactive USA, SVTIX USA, Punch Tab USA, Clarion India, Global Logic Ukraine, G5 Consulting South Africa, OnePixel South Africa, Springleap South Africa, Carver Media South Africa, Quirk South Africa, Sideman & Bancroft LLP USA, Shepstone & Wylie South Africa.

Thanks to the inspiring works of The Dalai Lama, Bill Gates, Warren Buffet, Deepak Chopra and George Soros for influencing my outlook in life.

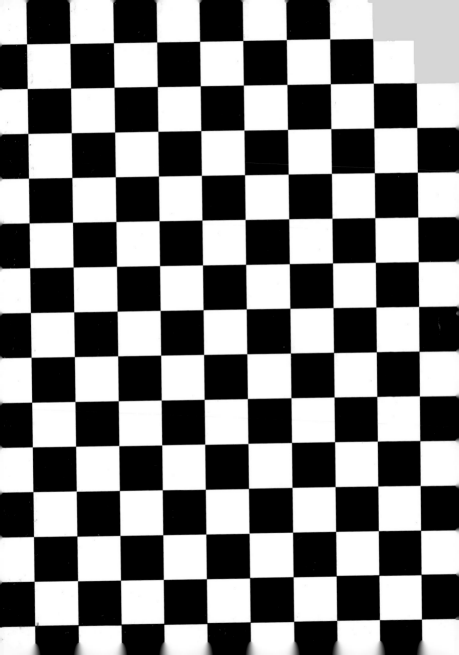